I0816786

THE LEGACY ADVENTURE

THE LEGACY ADVENTURE

SPEAK TO FUTURE GENERATIONS ABOUT THE THINGS THAT MATTER

TONY JEARY
The RESULTS Guy™

GREG VAUGHN
The LEGACY Guy

PUBLISHING

The Legacy Adventure

Published by RESULTS Faster! Publishing in Flower Mound, TX

Editing by Adept Content Solutions
Content Development by Nonie Jobe
Cover Design by Bryleigh Andrews

Printed in the United States of America

Contents

Introduction

Legacy is a canvas with your impact being painted on it day by day.

Tony Jeary

At the end of your life, what will people say about you?

When that time arrives, what difference will you have made on the lives of others, particularly in the lives of your family and the generations to come?

Putting it another way, what will be your legacy?

We believe legacy is much more than the money you make or the things you've achieved during your lifetime. A legacy, in fact, encompasses both the tangible and intangible elements you build during your time on this earth as well as what you leave behind, including your assets, accomplishments, values, and principles. **It represents the impact you make while you are here and the ways in which you are remembered after you are gone.** A legacy reflects your significance—your contribution to your community, your family, and society at large. It represents the enduring impact of your influence, actions, and values.

A legacy includes your financial assets, real estate, and private property; yet it also extends to any potential intellectual property (published works, print, music, poetry, courses, video, and other), knowledge, influence, and values. It encompasses your philanthropic endeavors, your cultural contributions, and your impact on relationships and communities. It may include financial bequests, certainly; and it could also include family traditions—maybe videos documenting family gatherings, scrapbooks or electronic files commemorating milestone events, or even things in print, favorite family stories, and pictures. **And, as you will see in part two of this book, a very powerful part of your legacy includes the blessings you invoke on your families.**

A well-lived life/legacy can inspire future generations, drive positive impact, and provide a road map for your offspring. And when you understand that and actively craft/plan your legacy, it allows you to live more intentionally, which fosters a stronger sense of purpose and most likely will leave a more meaningful imprint on the world.

Tony: Years ago, my family and I created a mission statement that has guided us on a daily basis; and this mission statement has contributed greatly to our family legacy:

We commit to doing together these 5 things as much as possible:	We will show everyone, including ourselves, these 5 qualities all the time:
1. Playing and having fun 2. Worshipping God 3. Teaching one another 4. Walking (exercise) 5. Helping others	1. Sharing 2. Supporting 3. Love 4. Being thankful 5. Being nice

I have also created a Personal Purpose Statement that guides me, as an individual, and is part of my personal legacy:

> The purpose of my life is to live each day happy and with the Lord, turning people toward God through my words and works; also being a great father, husband, and friend while giving to, improving, and serving all people.

Greg: My brother Steven got polio when he was eleven months old; and since this was before the Salk vaccine, he ended up severely affected. My dad didn't handle this well; he began to drink heavily and throw himself into his work, putting in eighteen hours a day, six and sometimes seven days a week at the community grocery store he ran.

Not long after my father's death, I was digging through his things in the garage when I came across his old tackle box. He was a rabid fisherman and loved it with a passion, but the tackle box had turned rusty with disuse. Once I finally pried it open, I found the usual refuse of a fisherman—worn out lures, dried salmon eggs, rubbery worms fused together, tangled line, and rusty hooks. None of it was any use to anyone anymore. I carried the box to a nearby garbage can and was preparing to toss it in when it suddenly occurred to me—this was all I had left of my father!

I began to weep. The only thing I had left from my dad—the same father who had never told me he loved me, never told me he was proud of me, never even hugged me—was an old tackle box and silence.

The tears suddenly turned to anger. I was angry at my father, angry at myself, angry at God. And I remember crying out to God, "This is all I get? I don't even have my father's signature!" For some silly reason known only to God, I was suddenly desperate for something written from my dad—something personal, something to hold on to.

Then God suddenly spoke to me. He said. "If you were to die today, what would be in the tackle box of your life? What would your children hold in their hands tomorrow that would let them know they were the treasures of your life?" I had to admit there was nothing.

When I went to bed that night, that question kept going over in my mind. I was sure my kids knew I loved them. Unlike my dad, I had told them countless times that I loved them and was proud of them. But something within me said that wasn't enough. I needed to do more. I needed to give them something tangible that they could keep long after I was gone.

And just like that, the thought popped into my head: *I need to leave my kids a blessing!*

We believe there is a series of great wins that can come from looking at our model we call the Four Quadrants of Life because we strongly believe your legacy is being built your whole life, in all four quadrants. It's important to note that each day, week, month and year of each quadrant, you are living your legacy; it may not be exactly in these years, but approximately. It helps to think about your life in each quadrant as we've presented it in this model. The model may not fit every person's life; yet it probably does fit the majority. The overall concept is that each of us is building our brand and reputation every day that goes by, and that brand and reputation rolls into our legacy. And it's not just when you're over sixty that you start building your legacy; you're building it all the time, and the sooner in life you can find your superpower (your genius, your niche), the more impact you can have on the world. Some people find it early, say in their twenties, and others find it later in life.

As you read through part one of this book, rather than reading it chronologically, you may want to start by reading the chapter that deals with the quadrant you're currently in. We highly recommend you read the remaining chapters at some point, though, for a couple of reasons:

1. If you're still in one of the first quadrants, you will want to know what to look for and how best to build your legacy as you progress through the later quadrants.
2. If you're in one of the latter quadrants, you may want to think about reading about the quadrants you've already gone through for the benefit of your kids; giving them these insights could be part of your legacy.

Either way, if you want to have a great legacy of your life on earth, you want to be really intentional.

Tony: When my daughters were six or seven years old, my wife and I asked them what kind of men they wanted to marry. Of course, at that age, they could only list one or two characteristics, so we helped them come up with a list of eleven qualities they would like to have in a husband. Then, almost every day until they went off to college, we talked and prayed with them about their becoming the kind of young ladies who would attract that kind of men to date and marry.

When my daughter Paige was in college, we hosted entrepreneur students from Baylor University to experience our entrepreneur mastermind sessions. In one of those sessions, we were discussing legacy and choosing the right mate; and I remember bragging about the fact that some of the guys who dated my daughters never got a second date because they didn't match the list. That's how intentional my daughters were about living that out. One of the students came to me after a session and said he was one of those young men. He said during the entire date with my daughter, Paige, she talked about me; and he could validate what I had said because he didn't get a second date. (As a disclaimer, I called Paige to ask her what was up with that, and she said it was not really an official date; it was a fraternity/sorority event—and that he was really a super nice guy.)

When my son-in-law Bret asked to marry my daughter Brooke, I told him he had a problem because few men had taken the energy I had to pour into their kids like I did. So there was a potential that my daughter could always be comparing him to me (especially during the first years of marriage), and that would be unfair to him for the rest of his life. I said it would be much better if I became number two, and I asked if he would let me pour into him. Then I said, "Let's start praying about your grandkids." He said, "You mean your grandkids?" I said, "No, yours. We're a generational family and we think long term."

Making that list in the first quadrant of our daughters' lives has had an enormous impact on our family's legacy! We are so blessed today to have two wonderful sons-in-law because my wife and I had the foresight in the second quadrant of our own lives to start building our legacy by having that initial conversation with our daughters.

Tony: *One of our traditions was to take our kids to a new country every year of their lives. As a family, we were always careful to give God thanks and express our gratitude for the blessings and favor we enjoyed from Him; and we would make a point to do that on the way to the airport each time we went to a new country.*

Part one of the book, which is from Tony's perspective, is made up of four chapters, one dedicated to each of the four common life quadrants. Here they are at a glance, including the approximate age of each quadrant.:

- Quadrant 1: **Learning** (1-25) – This phase is about education, personal growth and development, setting the foundation for future success, and really developing your *Life Philosophy.* (Some do this intentionally, yet most don't even have a clue; they are letting life guide them instead of designing their own life aligned with what they really believe and value.)

- Quadrant 2: **Earning** (26-50) – The focus shifts toward professional development and building financial ability and stability, and often toward marrying smartly (hopefully) and then starting and raising a family.
- Quadrant 3: **Reaping** (51-75) – This phase emphasizes harvesting the rewards of your focus the previous two quadrants—seeing you kids winning, potentially having grandkids, experiencing the world through travel, and enjoying wins from all the relationships you've built and, of course, from your financial net worth.
- Quadrant 4: **Returning** (76-100) – The focus shifts here toward giving back and sharing your wisdom with your family, your church, your associations, and/or your network. It also involves zeroing in on continuing good health habits so you can make a strong finish, leaving a lasting impact on future generations.

In part two of the book, which is given from Greg's perspective, we teach you what it means to bestow a blessing upon your children and other loved ones. We even teach you how to do it by introducing you to four powers you have at your disposal that can serve as instruments of the blessings you want to impart: the power of the written word, the power of the spoken blessing, the power of a visual legacy, and the power of prayer. And we share stories that show you what an amazing difference these blessings can make in the lives of those who receive them.

Greg: To put it politely, I'm not known for my "eloquence" in writing—never have been. (Just ask any of my teachers from either high school or college!) So how in the world was I going to pull off blessing my loved ones if I couldn't coherently string together two sentences in writing, much less have it grammatically correct? The answer came to me: Call your friends for help.

My group started out with fourteen of my close friends. These guys truly loved their kids, and giving them a blessing sounded like a great idea. Now we just needed to figure this thing out. None of us knew what an amazing adventure lay before us, but as a group, we had a mission statement: To leave a legacy of faith, hope, and love to our children and our children's children. Like Don Quixote in search of windmills, we set off into the unknown.

We started with writing a letter of blessing to our wives, and within a matter of weeks, strong marriages had been made stronger and marriages on the verge of collapse had begun to heal. Then we moved on to our kids. We decided we couldn't let any more time go by without writing to our children and giving them our blessing—and we experienced similar results of renewed relationships and healing. Then we wrote letters to our parents—both the living and the deceased—to honor them for everything they had done for us. (We included writing to those who had passed away so our children and grandchildren would know what they did to help shape us into the men we had become.) For those of us who had tough upbringings from one parent or another (or both), that was a hard thing to do. Suffice it to say that when we were finally able to write the letters, the blessings that came back to us were immeasurably greater than we gave.

Our final letters were just that—our final letters. I asked them, "What would you say if you could speak at your own funeral?" I encouraged them to express their love and affirmation to their families, and to fill their letters with the essentials of what they would want to leave them, their final thoughts, and the important truths they would want them to uphold after they were gone. When it comes time to write the final letter of your life, you want to write about the things that really matter. We all wrote our letters and put them in a special place for safekeeping until the time we leave this earth. (Of course, we have been sure to let someone in our family know about the letters and where they are.)

Mainly because of the excitement generated by these men's wives, our little group of fourteen men turned into 130 at the next meeting, then to 600 at the next. It was growing so exponentially that I formed an advisory board from my original group of fourteen men to help me make decisions in moving forward. Convinced that the local church should be the focus of our newly formed ministry, Letters from Dad, we decided the best way to further that focus was to establish large groups within each church that could then be broken down into smaller ones—**our Legacy Groups**. We're now in more than 4,000 churches worldwide.

It's now my great honor and privilege to serve a large and growing army of men called dads—an army of courageous fathers who have chosen to go on a mission. As a father, my assignment is clear and profound. It affects not only my wife and children, but generations not yet born.

When we were introduced by a great mutual friend, Peter Stuart, the profound affinity we both had for leaving a meaningful legacy struck a deep cord within us both. Greg had built an entire ministry around leaving a legacy of love to your family through blessings. I (Tony) had been working for many months to put together a book based on a seed that was planted in my head from my great friend and business partner, Peter Thomas, on the power of building a legacy in all four quadrants of your life. I now know why that book had not come together swiftly before I met Greg, as most typically do for me when I have a vision for a book. We were meant to author this book together.

Over the last three-and-a-half decades, I've worked with exceptional high achievers all over the world, including the presidents of some of the largest companies in the world, teaching them how to win, both personally and professionally, through my secret sauce of *Clarity*, *Focus*, and *Execution*. In the meantime, Greg has invested his career bringing heroes like Anne Frank and Susan B. Anthony to life through his Emmy-award-winning film series called *In Search of the Heroes* and building modern-day heroes by training men to win through his *Letters from Dad* program. He's also produced over 150 family video biographies that help people speak to future generations about the things that matter! These *A & E*-style movies have often featured high-profile clients like Zig Ziglar, Henry S. Miller (real estate titan), Coach Grant Teaff (Baylor University legend), Phil Romano (founder, Fuddruckers and Macaroni Grill), and Mabel Peters Caruth (philanthropist), that have enabled men and women to leave their families priceless firsthand accounts of their lives and legacies. In other words, we've both been about essentially the same thing—helping others live their very best lives and leave their very best legacies. We believe this book is an extension of our respective missions.

Fortuitously, Greg and I share another attribute: We both have a "Guy" moniker. For years, I've been known as the RESULTS Guy™, and Greg's well-earned title is the Legacy Guy. This form of casual and approachable branding positions us both as someone you can trust in the areas in which we've committed our lives to serving.

Subconscious desires are underlying drives and motivations that can influence our behavior and decision-making without our being fully aware of them. While there is no definitive list of basic subconscious desires, here are twenty that are common:

1. Survival - The desire to stay alive and protect yourself from harm
2. Security - The desire to feel safe and protected
3. Belonging - The desire to be part of a community or group
4. Love - The desire to be loved and accepted by others
5. Esteem - The desire to feel valued and respected
6. Self-actualization - The desire to reach your full potential
7. Power - The desire to have control or influence over others
8. Control - The desire to have control over your environment or circumstances
9. Freedom - The desire to have independence and autonomy
10. Curiosity - The desire to explore and learn new things
11. Novelty - The desire for new experiences and sensations
12. Comfort - The desire for physical and emotional comfort

13. Pleasure - The desire for enjoyable sensations or experiences
14. Social approval - The desire to be liked and accepted by others
15. Competition - The desire to win or outperform others
16. Justice - The desire for fairness and equality
17. Validation - The desire to be seen and understood by others
18. Connection - The desire for deep and meaningful relationships
19. Expression - The desire to express yourself creatively or authentically
20. Legacy - The desire to leave a lasting impact on the world

These desires may not follow a specific order, as different individuals may prioritize them differently depending on their unique experiences and circumstances.

Hopefully, you'll find many aha's in this book—perspectives about legacy you may have never thought of or that you're seeing in a different light. (Perhaps you already have in just these first few pages.) We encourage you to keep your eye out as well for epiphanies—ideas and concepts that may be life-changing for you as you give serious thought to intentionally building your legacy, starting in whatever quadrant you're in. It's not too early or too late to start your *Legacy Adventure* where you are so you can make the best impact possible on your family, friends, and colleagues for generations to come.

We've learned that we can make a vast difference in the lives of others by being more intentional, and so can you.

Tony: We're currently launching my 100th book, a coffee table book commemorating my first 99 works.

Several of the books we've published recently have ended up in trifectas with other books we've published. This book, for example, will be in a trifecta with my *Strategic Parenting* book (100 things my wife and I did intentionally to raise extraordinary adult children), along with a book called *Family Wealth* that I coauthored several years ago about sharing your values, principles and contacts with your kids. I had a man in my office recently discussing a partnership deal we are starting; and when I found out he had several children, I was excited to be able to hand him my *Strategic Parenting* book as a gift he wasn't expecting. All three books (including this one) have been written with the intention of giving them as gifts and of course selling them for others to give as gifts. I highly recommend that you read the other two books in conjunction with this one, as well as Greg's powerful best seller *Letters from Dad*.

INTRODUCTION VIPS

1. A legacy encompasses both the tangible and intangible elements you build during your time on this earth as well as what you leave behind, including your assets, accomplishments, values, and principles. It represents the impact you make while you are here and the ways in which you are remembered after you are gone.
2. A very powerful part of your legacy includes the blessings you invoke on your families.
3. A well-lived life/legacy can inspire future generations, drive positive impact, and provide a road map for your offspring. When you actively craft/plan your legacy, it allows you to live more intentionally, which fosters a stronger sense of purpose and most likely will leave a more meaningful imprint on the world.
4. There are four common quadrants of life:
    - Quadrant 1: **Learning** (1-25)
    - Quadrant 2: **Earning** (26-50)
    - Quadrant 3: **Reaping** (51-75)
    - Quadrant 4: **Returning** (76-100)

    Each day, week, month and year of each the Four Quadrants of Life you are living your legacy; and the sooner in life you can find your superpower, the more impact you can have on the world.

5. There is tremendous power in bestowing a blessing upon your children and other loved ones. You have four powers at

your disposal that can serve as instruments of the blessings you want to impart: the power of the written word, the power of the spoken blessing, the power of digital media, and the power of prayer.

PART ONE

Create Your Legacy in all Four Quadrants of Life

Note from Tony Jeary: My entire life has been about being intentional, as you will discover. I started goal setting and planning my life at the age of 17.

I've had five acts in my business life so far, each about a decade long: entrepreneuring, training, presenting as an expert, being *The RESULTS Guy*—an advisor to the world's top CEOs—and now, partnering with and scaling successful companies.

On the personal side, I've enjoyed a thirty-five-plus-year marriage and the joy of raising a family, including two amazing daughters and now grandchildren. My goal was always to become the president of my kids' fan club and pour parental privilege into my family like no other.

My resume is truly a blessing. God has allowed me to experience ups and downs like everyone. I've authored over 100 books, coached the presidents of some of the world's most recognized companies, and co-authored with both of my daughters. I've taken them to a new country every year of their lives and have poured love and support into them since the day they were born. I've prayed for their safety; their husbands; and, of course, their salvation. All of this is my legacy so far.

I invite you to click the QR code to watch and listen to the reasoning behind this book. I sincerely hope that through these pages—both mine and my coauthor Greg's—we positively impact your thinking, your life, and the generations that follow you.

Let's move forward—intentionally.

Tony Jeary

Please view Video Intro:

CHAPTER ONE

Quadrant 1—Learning (1–25)

A true legacy is built by living with purpose, passion, and persistence.

Tony Jeary

In the first quarter of your life, from the approximate ages of 1 to 25, you are typically in your formative years, focusing on learning and development. This period can best be described as the foundation-building stage, where you establish the building blocks of your education, life experiences, and what you believe to be true or not true. These foundational influences have a monumental impact on how you live your life and consequently play an enormous role in your legacy.

Parental Privilege

It is both my observation and my experience that the higher your *Parental Privilege* (the more your parents poured into you with love, exposure, opened doors, personal development, and modeling successful living), the higher your self-esteem and the more connections, experiences, and confidence you have. And the opposite is true as well. Those with a high *Parental Privilege* often excel more, and sometimes those with low *Parental Privilege* struggle their entire lives to believe in themselves.

Some extreme examples of people who had *Parental Privilege* are John Kennedy, who's dad was a United States Ambassador and married a governor's daughter, and Bill Gates.

Here are five things from Bill Gates' upbringing that contributed to his success:

1. Access to computers at a young age: Gates had access to computers at his school from a young age, which allowed him to develop his programming skills early on.
2. Entrepreneurial parents: Gates' parents were both successful entrepreneurs, which likely influenced his own entrepreneurial spirit.
3. Encouragement to pursue his interests: Gates' parents encouraged him to pursue his interests in computers and technology, even allowing him to drop out of Harvard to start Microsoft.
4. Exposure to business and finance: Gates' father was a successful lawyer, which exposed Gates to the world of business and finance from a young age.
5. Supportive family: Gates had a supportive family who believed in and nourished his abilities and encouraged him to pursue his passions.

As for John F. Kennedy, here are five factors that contributed to his success:

1. Privileged upbringing: Kennedy came from a wealthy and politically connected family, which provided him with opportunities and connections that helped him succeed.
2. Education: Kennedy received a top-notch education at elite institutions like Harvard and Stanford, which prepared him for a career in politics.
3. Military service: Kennedy's service in the Navy during World War II gave him a sense of discipline and leadership that served him well in politics.
4. Family support: Like Gates, Kennedy had a supportive family who encouraged him to pursue his ambitions and provided him with resources and connections.
5. Charisma and communication skills: Kennedy watched his father's personality, known for his charisma and ability to communicate effectively, which helped him learn to connect with so many and build support for his political campaigns.

I believe that even when *Parental Privilege* is lacking in some areas, it helps you compensate for any gaps. For example, as I was growing up I was told over and over as part of my *Parental Privilege,* "You can do it," "You're good with math," or "You're the best at [whatever was appropriate at the time]." There were some things, though, such as healthy eating, that were lacking in my *Parental Privilege;* my mom passed away obese. I became overweight as well; yet at the age of fifty I was blessed to realize I had to change my legacy because my kids were seeing me model wrong habits and I was adversely affecting the generations in my family. It took me four years to trim up, and since then I have authored four books on health. And now, my grandchildren call me Slim (a name I personally selected to positively affect our grandkids).

My legacy includes being voted best dressed in high school because of my dad's influence. On the other hand, I've not been good at spelling; so my whole life I've been admonished for being weak in written communication because of my many spelling errors. However, I wasn't concerned because I was focused on the keys to success my grandfather modeled for me, such as math and over-delivering service; I knew I could outsource spelling.

My grandfather only had an eighth-grade education; yet because of his *Parental Privilege*, he left a legacy of a great family and a stellar community brand, and he died a millionaire and was considered financially successful. His legacy largely affected my own, as he modeled discipline in every area, including work; he blessed me with many connections; and he greatly influenced how I think. Neither my dad nor my mom ever finished college; yet their *Parental Privilege* shaped them both and they were highly respected in the community, had no enemies and many friends, and led a very happy life. Both my parents and my grandparents provided a powerful model for me in how to raise a family. In fact, my favorite book to give away is a book I authored called *Strategic Parenting*, which gives 100 real and proven ideas every parent and grandparent should consider doing to raise extraordinary kids. This is all part of my legacy because of my *Parental Privilege.*

One factor that has a considerable effect on our success is something we call our *Belief Window*, and it is highly affected by *Parental Privilege* (or lack thereof). Our *Belief Window* contains principles that filter how we see the world and consequently make decisions. It includes everything we believe to be true, false, correct, incorrect, appropriate, inappropriate, possible, and impossible. Primarily, we get the principles on our window from our upbringing—our parents and teachers—during this first quadrant of life. However, we also get them from our experiences (e.g., sports, internships, and travel), our coaches, and our relationships (mostly our friends and their parents at this stage), as well as information we get from books, the internet, and other media. All of us are doing life right now the very best we can based on our principles, and it all started with our parents. [Note: Even if we had positive *Parental Privilege*, we have to be careful to make sure throughout our lifetimes that all the principles on our *Belief Windows* are true.]

As you can see, your legacy starts in Quadrant 1 and is heavily affected by your upbringing. Knowing that, you need to more carefully manage your own legacy by how you parent and grandparent, how you manage health habits at a young age, how you discover and strategically exploit your gifts and talents, and how you begin building and nourishing relationships.

In this first quadrant of life, you embark on a journey of self-discovery and personal/educational development. This phase, marked by exploration and growth, serves as a crucial foundation for establishing a purposeful and fulfilling future. To navigate this formative period successfully, consider the following key elements:

Education and Skills Development

During this quadrant, you need to focus on acquiring knowledge and abilities (which today includes how to have AI be your thinking partner) through various means, such as formal schooling, vocational training, and apprenticeships. Here are some ways my legacy (and/or my kids' legacy) was affected in these areas during the first quadrant:

Formal schooling: I hired a college coach for my oldest daughter to help guide the college years for my kids, since I had skipped college and missed that understanding.

Vocational training: I attended more seminars and workshops in my early twenties than anyone I personally know of. Why? I wanted knowledge faster than college could provide at the time.

Apprenticeships: My parents encouraged me to have multiple jobs in high school. (I had probably ten or more.) I considered each job an apprenticeship, as I learned a great deal from each one. (If you're still in this quadrant, please understand my strong opinions that strategic apprenticeships are huge. I encourage you to seek them out. If you're in another quadrant of your life, guide your family into strategic apprenticeships as well as self-directed learning as part of your legacy. AI is changing the learning options in a transforming way.)

It's crucial to identify and pursue an educational path that resonates with your passions and professional aspirations. Be proactive in seeking out resources and opportunities that enhance your learning experience and prepare you for the future.

I played out my legacy during my first quadrant leveraging my mathematical gifts and my ability to create rich relationships. I stopped formal higher education after taking nine hours of college during high school; yet I went on to double down on self-learning, studying an average of over two hours a day for forty years now! That's way more than most, which has positioned me to author over

100 books to date, many written and published just to give away to positively impact others' lives as part of my own legacy.

Embrace a growth mindset, acknowledging that making mistakes and facing challenges are integral parts of the learning process. Stay curious and open-minded as you broaden your understanding of the world and your place within it. By laying a strong foundation during this foundational stage, you will equip yourself with the tools necessary to create a meaningful and lasting legacy in the years to come.

Self-Discovery and Exploration

Dive into a diverse range of interests, and find your gifts. During this quadrant, most people find a job, some find a career, and a very few find their vocation—where they live all the way through Quadrant 4 using their God-given strengths, talents, and passions, and where they love every day because their work is like a hobby.

Embrace your opportunity during this quadrant to take strategic risks and a make a habit of learning from your mistakes, viewing them as essential stepping stones on your path to personal growth. By engaging in new experiences and pursuing your passions, you will cultivate a deeper understanding of your identity and forge a clear sense of purpose.

Leveraging Guidance and Mentorship

Consider in this quadrant that mentors change lives. (If you want a "wow" legacy, establish mentors everywhere!) A coach, who is a paid mentor, works well for building your legacy as well, yet not in all quadrants. Surround yourself with a supportive network of peers, mentors, and role models who can offer invaluable insights and guidance on your journey.

Utilize resources like my *Advice Matters* and *Rolodex* books to expand your thinking and to build and maintain meaningful connections, as they will play a pivotal role in shaping your character and fostering your growth.

Cultivating Resilience

Develop the emotional fortitude and adaptability necessary to overcome challenges and setbacks with unwavering determination. Life's not fair; yet you can cultivate emotional intelligence and a growth mindset by understanding that obstacles are inevitable but surmountable. By honing your resilience, you will emerge stronger and better equipped to navigate life's complexities. Learn how to leverage serendipity.

Establishing Purpose-Driven Goals

Set realistic and achievable goals that align with your core values and aspirations. For a well-rounded approach, consider incorporating goals related to acquiring, sharing, giving, experiencing, and becoming through personal growth, as inspired by my *Designing Your Own Life* framework. By thoughtfully designing your life around purposeful objectives, you will create a compelling vision for your future, fueling your motivation to pursue your dreams.

The Learning Quadrant is a transformative period in your life, offering rich opportunities for self-discovery and personal development. The foundation of your legacy obviously starts here.

As you progress into Quadrant 2, the Earning Quadrant, your legacy will begin to take on deeper meaning. You'll want to become even more intentional about building the brand and reputation that will serve you and your family best throughout your generations.

CHAPTER ONE READER RESPONSE

For those who are still in Quadrant 1:

1. On a scale of 1 to 5, with 5 being the highest, what level of *Parental Privilege* (your parents have poured into you with love, exposure, opened doors, personal development, and modeling successful living) do you feel you have experienced?

   a. If you rated your level as 3 or above, name five things you can intentionally do to capitalize on the advantages you have been given:

   1. ______________________________
   2. ______________________________
   3. ______________________________
   4. ______________________________
   5. ______________________________

   b. If you are below a level 3, name five things you can intentionally do to compensate for any areas you feel you are lacking in:

   1. ______________________________
   2. ______________________________
   3. ______________________________
   4. ______________________________
   5. ______________________________

2. How can you enhance your education and skill development while you are still in this quadrant?

____

____

____

____

3. List what you believe to be your strengths, talents, and passions.

____

____

____

____

4. Find at least one mentor who has been successful in an area you are interested in pursuing.
5. Set at least one goal in each of the following areas:

   To Have: ____

   To Share: _______________________________________

   To Give: ____

   To Experience: ___________________________________

   To Become: ______________________________________

For those who have children who are still in Quadrant 1:

1. On a scale of 1 to 5, with 5 being the highest, what level of *Parental Privilege* (you have poured into your children with love, exposure, opened doors, personal development, and modeling successful living) do you feel you provided for your children?

   a. If you scored a 3 or above, name three things you can intentionally do to help your children capitalize on the advantages they have been given:

   1. ______________________________

   2. ______________________________

   3. ______________________________

   b. If you scored below a 3, name three things you can intentionally do to compensate for any areas you feel they were lacking in:

   1. ______________________________

   2. ______________________________

   3. ______________________________

2. How can you help your children go to the next level in their education and skill development while they are in this quadrant?

   ____

   ____

   ____

3. What role can you play in helping your children find one or more mentors while they are in this quadrant?

   ____

   ____

   ____

4. How can you help your children achieve their goals while they are in this quadrant?

   ____

   ____

   ____

CHAPTER ONE **VIPS**

1. Typically, the higher your *Parental Privilege*, the higher your self-esteem and the more connections, experiences, and confidence you have. Therefore, you need to more carefully manage your own legacy by how you parent and grandparent, how you manage health habits at a young age, how you discover and strategically exploit your gifts and talents, and how you begin building and nourishing relationships.
2. Embrace your opportunity during this quadrant to take strategic risks and make a habit of learning from your mistakes, viewing them as essential steppingstones on your path to personal growth. By engaging in new experiences and pursuing your passions, you will cultivate a deeper understanding of your identity and forge a clear sense of purpose.
3. Surround yourself with a supportive network of peers, mentors, and role models who can offer invaluable insights and guidance on your journey.
4. Set realistic and achievable goals that align with your core values and aspirations. For a well-rounded approach, consider incorporating goals related to having, sharing, giving, experiencing, and becoming through personal growth.

CHAPTER TWO

Quadrant 2—Earning (26–50)

Your legacy is not about the titles you hold; rather, it's about the people you inspire and the lives you impact.

Tony Jeary

Most people generally move from the Learning Quadrant to the Earning Quadrant somewhere in their mid-twenties. Some may start a little earlier, some a little later, depending on their life experiences to this point. The main idea is that you want to make sure you're thinking about your legacy in terms of providing the economic stability and direction for the roles you might play in your life.

This quadrant is really where you start the journey of discovering what your values are and who want to become for the rest of your life. You don't want to spend your life waiting for things to happen; you want to become the actualizer—the author—and design your own life (again, see my book of that name), making it unfold the way you want it.

Ideally, when you're in your early twenties and in your education years (Quadrant 1), you're discovering what you're passionate about, or where your genius (superpower) is that we mentioned in the introduction. Hopefully, you're playing that out in Quadrant 2 and earning a ton of money using that gift (or those gifts). Sadly, many people don't really search for that sweet spot, and consequently they seldom develop an intentionality about who they want to become. We believe you'll find happiness once you discover your superpower and learn how to use it in order to fulfil your purpose.

My superpower is helping people win. I love what I do, and every day is like a weekend to me. When I first entered Quadrant 2 in my personal life, though, I had just gone through a disastrous financial dip. I went insolvent and needed to reboot my economic engine as an entrepreneur. I decided to reflect back on my learning years, during which I discovered there's a lot of power in imparting advice, and I set my vision on that.

It took me several years to get my momentum going; then in 1991, I got a phone call from my mentor telling me that Lee Iacocca was leaving Chrysler, which was on its last leg at the time. He said they were hiring many consultants to help turn it around and that they could perhaps use someone with my expertise. I went for an interview, and they hired me. That one opportunity turned into 156 more assignments and millions of dollars, which was the catalyst that rebooted the earning platform of my life. It also built my brand and opened doors for me to go on and coach the president of the third largest company at the time, Ford Motor Company. From there, I became the coach to the president of Sam's Club, and that led to my coaching Kiuchi-San, who was the president of Seiyu Corporation in Japan, which was acquired by Walmart. From there I coached the presidents of Walmart Canada and Walmart

Mexico, and eventually Walmart US and on to the CEO over all of Walmart—at that time, the largest company in the world.

In our earning years, my wife and I were able to be really disciplined in the way we worked together to build a legacy as a highly respected and admired couple. We did not necessarily become a "power couple," per se, although some I have coached have aspired to and achieved that status; and it's a powerful concept that can maximize your earning years.

This quadrant was my career-and brand-development years, which is typical for someone in their late twenties and thirties. During those years, you should be looking at the kind of legacy you want to build with the people and customers you support and how you, as a leader, want to grow the people under you as they're coming up through the ranks.

Of course, these are also the years during which most people begin a family. My wife and I wanted to wait to start a family until after our earnings were in full motion again, and we eventually had two beautiful daughters. At that point, we were purposefully into how we could build a great family together, with my driving the earning side and her pouring more into our family. We built our legacy in such a way that our kids always felt loved; they always knew our intention was, to quote my daughter, to "always make them feel like we had our arm around them to support them."

That's a great place to be in your career development years—not losing sight of the importance of pouring into your kids and having that balance between work and family. A lot of people miss that. I often tell my clients, "You can always make more money, but you can't relive those years of raising your family." So during these earning years, I not only sought out mentorships that would help me with my career; I also sought out those that would help us grow our family well.

I adopted three great men—Bill Arnold, Steve Dulin, and Lamar Smith—as my family mentors; all three happened to have daughters ten or fifteen years older than ours, so that meant they were half a generation ahead of us. During those earning years, they diligently poured into us. I encourage you, whether you're reading this as a younger person in your earning years or whether you're older and looking back at your own kids who are in this quadrant of their lives, to be thinking about the value of family mentorships.

It's very important that you build financial stability during these years. What does that look like? It's developing not only earning capacity, but good money management habits as well, where you begin saving or building toward your future. Many people burn through what they're making and don't put money "over the fence" for the next quadrants of their lives. Ideally, you can build enough financial wealth to eventually, maybe even one day soon, be able to make money without working (twenty-four hours a day) because you've invested smartly—whether that's in a business, in public ownership of companies, or in a variety of other options. Financial stability is such a powerful asset to have in your legacy so your kids can see you're not struggling for money. It's great to show them just the opposite—that you are disciplined with your money and are able to pour that into them.

Financial Security

Financial security comes from effectively budgeting; managing your money; building your credit; saving; and, of course, investing to put yourself in a position to be making money in your sleep. It often occurs toward the end of Quadrant 2 as you move into the third quadrant of your life, where you're continuing to earn money while simultaneously reaping some freedom as a result of the discipline you had in Quadrant 2.

Achieving financial security requires maintaining good money management habits—period! Making money, of course, is a basic necessity for creating security, well-being, and wealth—whether you work for someone else or yourself. No matter what you're doing as "work," make sure your work ethic is one that seeks to always do more than is expected so you will always be maximizing your opportunities. Those who have a strong work ethic typically fall into the category of a higher earner, and they are often also better at money allocation. They budget their money better for the things they need, and they also end up saving more than their counterparts.

No matter how much money you make, if you are a poor manager of how you allocate that money, it will be virtually impossible to create wealth. The percentages of things you allocate money for may vary over time, depending on how aggressively you want to build your wealth; yet as a good rule of thumb, approximately 50 percent of your income should go to essentials like housing, food, transportation, and utilities. Another 20 percent should be set aside for saving and investing, which includes savings plans, debt payments, and rainy-day funds, as well as long-term savings. And for those who following the teachings of the Bible, another 10 percent should be set aside for tithing.

The last 20 percent should be for personal. These are non-essential luxuries that enhance your lifestyle and could be given up if needed, such as gym memberships, pedicures, housekeepers or property maintenance, trips to the coffee shop, cable TV, or additional charitable contributions. Depending on your income, this is a great place to reduce your spending and add to your savings plan to better contribute to growing wealth and surplus.

Deferred Gratification

To win the money game, one of the most important things you can do is practice delayed gratification—waiting until later for something you desire today. That doesn't necessarily mean you need to remove that want from your radar; it just means that sometimes prioritizing and working toward a secure future means deferring some of those things now that you really want to do. This could mean keeping your car an extra year or two, or even buying a good used one instead of a new one. It could also mean being out of balance for a period of time in your work/life balance (smartly) to build financial reserves. Once you have the reserves, you can reevaluate.

If you are an employee (or even if you work for yourself), a type of deferred gratification is to contribute to some type of qualified plan like an IRA or an SEP contribution. You may also contribute to a defined benefit plan if you are self-employed. As an employee, you often receive matching funds, so the amount of compounding grows even more. We call that a *Force Multiplier*, especially when you start it early in your career. First, you practice deferred gratification by saving the initial dollars; then your employer matches at least some level of those funds; and finally, you make interest on both the first and second phase, which compounds dramatically over time. Your money is multiplied beyond the normal interest made.

Another key to achieving financial security is managing your debt and credit habits. Budgeting is a key to truly managing your money because it can help you allocate and save your money more efficiently and more quickly.

Creating and committing to a budget will reduce overspending, and yet you can still allow yourself some freedom to purchase things that are important to you—even if they are not necessities. You can make the rules. However, it is important to be realistic and look at both the short-term and the long-term repercussions of your spending habits.

Do you spend as much as you make? Do you spend more than you bring in? Are you going deeper into debt to purchase things that are non-essentials? If you answered yes to any of these questions, you definitely want to create a plan for spending that includes saving and allowing for unexpected fluctuations in cash flow. Paying down your debt and increasing your savings will reduce your stress and allow you freedoms you are not currently enjoying. Use your budget to help you know when to stop spending. A budget should be used to consistently move toward spending less than you earn.

Having a budget can also help you reach your personal and financial goals faster. You can shift your money spending to the things that are the most important to you, whether it is reducing debt, purchasing a home, buying a new car, or perhaps travel. Your budget acts as a strategy and a plan that will help you get results.

Mostly, a budget puts you in control. It allows you to prioritize your spending and track how you're doing according to your plan. It also allows you to make adjustments. It is an intentional tool for being accountable for your own future by allocating your money in such a way that will create surplus.

Once you've learned to budget your money, the next step is to look at saving and investing strategies. Let's first review the three things it takes to have savings: discipline, deferred gratification, and a plan. You need to keep enough in your savings account for your rainy-day fund and emergencies. After that, a savings account can have enough surplus to begin diversifying in investments and then eventually building wealth.

Simply stated, when you have disposable income and extra money, you need to decide what you are going to do with it. Some traditional financial advisors might advise you to throw it into a savings account. It's a rainy-day fund, and it should be kept in short term investments. It's there in case of emergency. The size of that should be enough to live for three months, six months, or a year—it's a personal preference, depending on what makes you feel both comfortable and confident. Once you've built up your reserves, it's time to think about and actually take action on investing using your surplus.

The goal is to get to surplus—lots of it. Anything below the line of surplus allows you to begin building toward wealth. Surplus is excess, and with that excess, you can set aside savings for a rainy-day emergency fund. Once you have your desired amount set aside for emergencies, you are ready to invest.

We don't need to get complicated here. As of this writing, interest rates are fairly low; and if you truly don't need this money for a long time, you need to just go buy a low-cost exchange-traded money market fund that represents the market. Let me give you a very telling perspective. Only one third of active money managers beat the market every year, and it's not the same third every year. Did you get that? Only one third of active money managers beat the market every year, and it's not the same third every year. That means that in choosing a safe, index-based mutual fund, you will be better off than two thirds of the money managers all the time. That's a pretty bold statistic.

Another facet of financial security is planning for retirement and long-term financial goals, and that includes generating estate planning and wills. One of the mistakes we see many make is lack of proper estate planning—looking at all the right instruments you need to put in place that would give you the mental assurance that you have things well thought out and documented. And the younger you are when you do this, the better. You should begin thinking about creating wills and trusts when you start having a family, really, because life is uncertain. It's also smart to plan your final arrangements during this quadrant— determine whether you will be an organ donor; make your burial or cremation decisions; purchase your burial plot, as appropriate; plan your funeral as far as possible; and possibly even write your obituary. These actions are all part of your legacy adventure.

In our case, we were determined even during those earning years to take our kids to a new country every year of their lives. We wanted that to be part of our legacy, and we wanted our kids to really appreciate what that looked like. At the same time, we were careful not to overspend, as we wanted to maintain financial stability. We had been broke once, and we never wanted to go there again; we learned from our mistakes at a very young age. In fact, one of my biggest learnings during my twenties was not to cross collateralize everything, as I had done earlier. I learned to build my income-earning potential and put the surplus from that over the fence and smartly invest it so I could be passively jumping up a notch or two. By doing that, I was able to improve my work/life balance.

The last thing you want is to have a legacy that makes your kids feel like you poured into your business too much and not enough into them. On the flip side, though, you don't want them to feel that you didn't pour enough into your business or professional life to make sure you were earning enough money to provide a good/positive lifestyle for them; establishing those work/life balance boundaries goes both ways.

I was blessed in my own situation to have my parents and grandparents model doing what they loved (entrepreneurship) and getting paid for it, even back during those years. They were real testimonies to the fact that we can actually be living in our vocation. That's a really great place to be in your legacy—to model for your own kids, but to show to other people you're influencing as well. Your legacy is not just for your kids; it's also for other people you lead who are watching to see if you, as their leader, are making their lives better by intentionally pouring into them. I believe an important piece of the work/life balance is to make sure you're giving back what God has blessed you with, to make it even more impactful.

Networking should be another intentional aspect of this time period between the ages of 26 and 50. This is when you start really building and nourishing rich relationships. (See my book, *Rich Relationships, Rich Life.*) It's easier to do this today than ever before, with all the different software products and so many options available on your phone. There are numerous ways to easily build V cards and capture pictures, and of course social media plays a huge part in nourishing connections today. I believe most people adopt social media now with a full-steam-ahead kind of thinking.

Networking and building relationships can be initiated electronically from social media; they can also be generated from your church or from attending the right events and joining the right organizations. Part of your legacy obviously evolves from who you hang around; so it's important to carefully and strategically choose who you invest time with and to make sure those people are influencing you positively.

Another intentional aspect of this quadrant should be personal growth and development. Obviously, this is of huge importance for me, since the books I author fall inside that genre—primarily on the side of business, yet with a few on the personal side; both areas of growth are important. While you're working to advance your career, you should be developing your personal growth as well—including in the area of parenting. In addition to finding mentors to help us grow and develop in this area, we studied how to be exceptional parents by watching videos and podcasts and reading parent magazines. I ask you to consider modeling what we did—doing whatever it takes to intentionally grow yourself in every way—both professionally and personally (in every quadrant).

These earning years, then, become a balance act of staying engaged in your career/investments, ensuring you're maximizing your full earning potential by building your brand and your connections, being disciplined in building that nest egg, working well with and leading other people, and becoming the best person you can be (including as a parent). In this quadrant, between the ages of 26 and 50, is when you put a lot of your effort into leveraging the learning you acquired in your first quadrant. And above all, you want to enjoy the journey by making sure you have good work/life balance. Focus on these areas, and you'll have more long-term success.

CHAPTER TWO READER RESPONSE

For those who are still in Quadrant 2:

1. From the 60 values listed below, choose the top ten that you believe will guide you for the rest of your life; then prioritize your top ten.

1. Affection	21. Friendship	41. Personal Brand
2. Alignment	22. Fun	42. Personal Improvement
3. Altruism	23. Generosity	43. Personal Salvation
4. Appearance	24. Genuineness	44. Philanthropy
5. Appreciated	25. Happiness	45. Power
6. Attitude	26. Harmony	46. Productivity
7. Cleanliness	27. Health	47. Recognition
8. Congruence	28. Honesty	48. Respect
9. Contentment	29. Humility	49. Results
10. Cooperation	30. Inner Peace	50. Romance
11. Creativity	31. Inspiration	51. Routine
12. Education	32. Intimacy	52. Security
13. Effectiveness	33. Joy	53. See the World
14. Efficiency	34. Knowledge	54. Simplicity
15. Fairness	35. Lifestyle	55. Solitude
16. Faith	36. Loved	56. Spiritual Maturity
17. Fame	37. Loyalty	57. Status
18. Family	38. Motivation	58. Wealth
19. Financial Security	39. Openness	59. Winning
20. Freedom	40. Organization	60. Wisdom

2. What do you believe is your "superpower"—what you are most passionate about—that will drive the fulfillment of your purpose in life?

____

____

3. Describe the kind of legacy you want to build with the people you support and how you, as a leader, want to grow the people under you as they're coming up through the ranks.

____

____

____

____

4. Describe the legacy you want to build for your family and how you want to be remembered after you are gone.

____

____

____

____

5. On a scale of 1 to 5, with 5 being the highest, rate yourself on where you currently are in achieving financial security for your family: _____ If you are at any level lower than 5, list five things you can do to drive toward the goal of financial security:

    1. ____________________________________
    2. ____________________________________
    3. ____________________________________
    4. ____________________________________
    5. ____________________________________

6. List three ways you can develop your personal growth:

   Personally (Be sure to consider finding a mentor for guidance in parenting your children):

   1. ______________________________
   2. ______________________________
   3. ______________________________

   Professionally:

   1. ______________________________
   2. ______________________________
   3. ______________________________

7. List three ways you will build (or continue building) your relationship network:

   1. ______________________________
   2. ______________________________
   3. ______________________________

For those who have children who are still in Quadrant 2:

1. How can you support your child(ren) in living their values?

   ____

   ____

   ____

   ____

2. How can you support your child(ren) in developing their "superpower"?

____

____

____

3. What kind of support can you provide in helping your child(ren) build their legacy:

   Personally: _______________________________________

   ____

   ____

   Professionally: ____________________________________

   ____

   ____

4. What can you do to support your child(ren) as they drive toward financial security?

____

____

____

CHAPTER TWO VIPS

1. The main idea in the Earnings Quadrant is to make sure you're thinking about your legacy in terms of providing the economic stability and direction for the roles you might play in your life. You should be looking at the kind of legacy you want to build with the people and customers you support and how you, as a leader, want to grow the people under you as they're coming up through the ranks.
2. It's crucial during those years to not lose sight of the importance of pouring into your kids and having that balance between work and family. You can always make more money, but you can't relive those years of raising your family.
3. Building financial stability during these years involves developing both earning capacity and good money management habits, where you begin saving or building toward your future. Ideally, you can build enough financial wealth to eventually be able to make money without working (twenty-four hours a day) because you've invested smartly.
4. Networking should be another intentional aspect of this time period, when you start really building and nourishing rich relationships. Part of your legacy obviously evolves from who you hang around; so it's important to carefully and strategically choose who you invest time with and to make sure those people are influencing you positively.
5. While you're working to advance your career, you should be developing your personal growth as well—including in the area of parenting.

CHAPTER THREE

Quadrant 3—Reaping (51–75)

Legacy is not a destination;
it's a journey of moments, memories, and impact.

Tony Jeary

As you build your ideal life through reflection and intentionally leave an impactful legacy, you want to make every year and every quadrant of your life count. Ideally, you want to be so intentional that each quadrant builds on the previous one and you are constantly living your best year ever, over and over—for yourself, for your family, and for all those your legacy will impact.

As your life continues through each quadrant, you want to continually study what matters most and take conscious actions accordingly. The third quadrant, called Reaping, should encapsulate many wins—like more flexibility of your time and perhaps even more intentional altruism, whereby you are impacting lives to another level while you're enjoying the life you've set up for yourself.

As for me, I'm constantly working on things like my "Morning Twenty-Seven"— twenty-seven things I do each day when I wake up. I'm working on authoring more books—I've refined the process and built a "wow" team; and because books can go where you can't go and stay longer than you can stay, I can have a huge impact on how I can help others.

I do things like carefully choose one or two interns for the summer and have them join my team, which impacts their lives forever. In fact, read this excerpt from a mini-book written by Riley Page about his ninety-day experience as an intern working under my leadership and the leadership of our team.

> Working closely with Tony Jeary and other leaders in the organization gave me a front-row seat to effective leadership. Tony's ability to inspire and influence others was evident in every interaction. I observed how he communicated his vision, motivated his team, and made strategic decisions. These experiences taught me the importance of leadership in achieving organizational goals and creating a positive work environment. Tony's emphasis on continuous learning and improvement resonated with me, encouraging me to seek new knowledge and constantly refine my skills.
>
> Critical thinking became an essential part of my role. I was often tasked with analyzing situations, making reasoned decisions, and solving problems creatively. Detailed note-taking during Tony's instructions was crucial for remembering tasks and deadlines, helping me manage my responsibilities more effectively, and ensuring I met expectations. Time management and multitasking were also vital skills I developed; balancing multiple projects and priorities taught me to be organized, proactive, and efficient in my work.
>
> My summer at Tony Jeary International was more than just an internship; it was a transformative experience. The lessons

> I learned, both professional and personal, have prepared me for future challenges and opportunities. As I continue my journey at the University of Oklahoma and beyond, these experiences will remain a cornerstone of my growth and success. The skills, insights, and values I gained will serve as a foundation for my future endeavors, helping me navigate the complexities of the professional world with confidence and resilience.

I look at how I can be a better leader and intentionally grow the thinking and success of each of my close team members. I look at my partnerships and how I can contribute to their achieving more of their goals. And, of course, I look at my family every day and think about how I can positively nourish their happiness. That includes being smart about opening doors for them by sharing my relationships and connecting them with my contacts, which can truly pay big dividends for them. (I've been extremely intentional about doing this for them since they were very young.) I also think about how I can model successful living and my health regiment to them and to other people, loving and nourishing all those I touch. (Again, see my book, *Rich Relationships, Rich Life*.)

By the time you cross over into your fifties and move into Quadrant 3, you have had many life experiences, ups and downs, and twists and turns, many of which have made you better and allowed you to navigate more intentionally. As an *Elegant Solution* (doing one activity and accomplishing several objectives), I like to maximize every day I live and at the same time look back at every day, every week, every month, and every year and be happy that I'm reaping the rewards of the many relationships I've built, the home I've designed, and my life's entire set up. Also at the same time, I enjoy having a positive impact on peoples' lives through my words and works.

Every year, I look forward to planning my goals for the next year—where I'm going to travel, who I'm going to meet, what I'm going to learn, how I'm going to do my best as each day goes by. Then at the end of each year I can truly reflect back and say, *This was the best year ever because I've become a better person, I've become more impactful, and I've experienced an incredible year.*

Ideally, you've been effective with your finances during your Earning Quadrant, meaning you've been diligent in building a legacy for your kids and others who are watching how you earn, save, and invest money, and, of course, how you spend it in relationship to how much you make. If you've done this successfully, you can move into this next quadrant in an optimized position to reap some of the financial security you've built.

One of the things I wanted to model as part of my legacy for my kids as they came into their adult years was to show them how good discipline on our part over the years would put us in a position to be able to support them in their college years. My son-in-law, a fantastic man, is in medical school; of course, delayed gratification comes with that vocation, as it pays off much later down the road. Being in a position to support them as a couple as they begin raising their family is really a reaping moment. And having a beautiful home my adult kids and my grandkids can come visit and feel the love my wife and I have for them is certainly a reaping moment as well. All this comes from practicing good stewardship in the first two quadrants.

Although financial security is certainly one of the benefits you enjoy in the Reaping Quadrant, we believe it also involves aspects of personal fulfillment, which includes altruism and community involvement as well as health and wellness.

Personal Fulfillment

Something that's very fulfilling to me personally—and it falls under both the reaping and building-my-legacy categories—is intentionally looking for what's important to my grown kids. I enjoy having conversations with them about their goals and aspirations and seeing how I can open a door for them, give them an inside perspective, or share a story, and in the process really feel valued as a mentor to them. There's an altruistic win that comes from helping and positioning your own kids and launching them into the world, and, of course, pouring into other family members (perhaps your grandkids) as well.

In fact, just last week I had a teaching moment with my two granddaughters. They weren't sharing their dolls like they should; so I had an impromptu talk with my oldest one about how they were going to be sisters their entire life, and that sharing needed to be part of their game plan. She actually responded better than I expected. So I asked my kids if they would consider our creating a code of conduct for our family, now that we're expanding under my patriarchism. I suggested that we expand on the mission statement we started when they were four and five (which I shared in the introduction). One item in the code of conduct might say that, as a family member, we're going to share and make sure we're helping the other family members win. That might be one of, say, five action items we list, and that code of conduct could become a valuable part of our legacy.

People occasionally ask me about our family traditions. One tradition for us is to have beautiful Christmas experiences and birthday dinners. Another tradition for our family is vision boarding; we enjoyed doing that together as my kids were growing up. Another has been doing an appreciation or branding exercise around the dinner table, where we write down something we appreciate about each person on separate cards and pass them around the table so everyone can write something on each person's card. Then we read the cards aloud and feel loved and appreciated by what everyone has said. Something my dad passed down to me, which I consider a tradition, is always looking at how you can help people win. Passing down your family traditions is an important part of your legacy.

I look forward to planning vacations two or three times a year with my kids and grandkids and then two, three, or four times a year with my wife, as we did this year. We planned ahead and went to Jamaica and enjoyed rest and rejuvenation time on the beach as well as beautiful dinners, and we sent pictures back to our family. In taking vacations like this, I believe we're modeling what our kids or even you might want to do in this third quadrant of life.

Lifelong learning is a giant deal to me, and I believe it can and probably should be part of anyone's legacy. Have you kept learning, or have you stopped? I look for learning experiences, including visiting museums, and I love having the economic means to hire tour guides to walk us through the museums. This year, my wife and I invested three full days in Washington, DC; and even though we had both been there many times before, we enjoyed those three days of learning more in depth about the constitution and art history from various countries. And we were able to send back pictures and videos to our family to sharpen their gratitude and appreciation for being Americans and keep them motivated to be great citizens.

Many people in this third quadrant have positioned their home(s) to be a place they really enjoy, and yet sometimes they stay so busy they don't have time to enjoy them. We like to lounge around in our home because we've set it in such a beautiful and peaceful environment. We live in a top-level condo in a tower overlooking a lake, and we have six balconies where we can enjoy beautiful sunrises and sunsets and invest quality time with friends and family. I built a man cave in my six-car garage (it's quite large), which includes a gym. I enjoy working out there, where I always have a flipchart handy for writing and brainstorming whatever I'm working on. Sometimes it's a book, or it may be an article or a video. Perhaps you have different art forms or hobbies you may enjoy during these reaping years. Being able to reap the rewards of the setup you've created serves as a great model for others.

I am really enjoying my condo-living lifestyle my wife and I have set up as part of our reaping years, and at the same time I'm enjoying the relationships we have with our wonderful neighbors. Sometimes we go on special dinner dates with them, and we've even done double-date traveling with couples we're close to in the tower. We had always wanted to visit the Holy Land, so two years ago we invested time and planning into a beautiful trip there. We enjoyed so many rewards there and took many pictures, and part of our legacy is that we've been able to use it as a semi-ministry tool as we've encouraged others to do the same (of course, when the political climate in the area makes sense to do so). This coming year, we're planning a beautiful trip to Rome with the same couple; and since we've been researching cool restaurants and great experiences to have once we get there, we're able to reap the exciting energy of planning such a trip now. I encourage you to do the same in this quadrant of your life.

My personal philosophy is grounded in being in God's will. I get much fulfillment from praying consistently that God will expand my territory (as Jabez did in 1 Chronicles 4:10), and that I will then impact others from that standpoint. As I mentioned previously, one of my personal mantras is to live every day like it's a weekend—

where you can't tell the difference between work and play because you've built a life where they are one and the same.

As I alluded to in chapter 2, I believe you can have a job, a career, or a vocation. You want the third option, which is a life by design. When you find your vocation, everyday work efforts fall into your sweet spot and you love your professional life so much that you literally just want more of the same. I recommend to my clients that they define their passions and what makes them happy, and then see if they can pull from that list to find or create their vocation. My list is: God, wisdom, planning, simplicity, freedom, altruism, health, travel, history, organization, being well dressed, the outdoors, sunshine, my kids, style, blossoming, being serene, having connections, growing, sharing, having fun, client success, and facilitation (interacting with and pulling the best out of people). I am reaping the rewards of my very fulfilling vocation, which makes room for everything on that list.

Hopefully, by the time you've reached this quadrant, you've discovered what you're passionate about and you're also enjoying the rewards of building a vocation around them. Everyone has their own interests and their own desires, and ideally your efforts have been in line with your personal values. If you've achieved the kind of success we've been talking about and have been about building your legacy during the first two quadrants of your life, you've obviously known what your values were and aligned your goals with those values. Your action plan had to have included your values-based strategy, or you would not have been able to endure for the long haul.

For years, I believed and taught others that their ultimate goal should be balance, which for me involved managing six areas of life: finances, health, home life, education, social life, and spirituality. (Some people limit it to fewer areas, and others include as many as twelve.) I have come to realize over the years, though, that this approach is wrong. It's not about balancing these areas in individual ways; rather, it's about practicing *managed balance.* It's about taking a step back to see what areas need more attention and what areas need less. If a family member is ill, for example, you may need to throw other areas of your life out of balance to take care of them. If you're in your early twenties and in Quadrant 1 of your life, you may need to zero in on your education, which might make it difficult to socialize or see your family as much as you'd like. And in Quadrant 2, you may want to double down on making a financial surplus by working more to build for your future.

By the time you get to Quadrant 3, your hobbies typically play a larger role in your life. I am currently in this quadrant, and I've personally taken on two hobbies that produce a dual win for me. One is writing books. I believe books can go where you can't go and can stay longer than you can stay, and I prefer investing my time in crafting a book any time over playing a game of golf. That's not for everyone, of course; yet that gives me a great deal of personal fulfillment.

My second hobby is my health. I am investing a ton of my time in training and working out to ensure I'm doing the right things to minimize health risks and maximize living at the ultimate health level. (We'll talk more about this later in this chapter.)

Personal fulfilment obviously includes enjoying life experiences as well. Along that line, a third hobby for me is travel. I've traveled millions of miles for business to over 50 countries, so travel today is less for business and more for luxury and enjoyment. As I mentioned, my wife and I enjoy going to museums and exploring the world, so we are able reap those life experiences during this quadrant of our lives.

For most people, practicing altruism and giving back plays a huge role in personal fulfilment. I like to call it "helping others win," and it's one of my very favorite things to do. The quality of helping others be champions or win more is truly a "wow" factor that can not only springboard you to success in life; it can also bring you much more fulfilment than you can get from virtually anything else.

In fact, this one is really personal for me. Having a legacy of helping others win is something I strive for every day. I'm at a point in my life where I can enjoy the fruit of my labor; yet that doesn't mean I'm slowing down, by any means! If anything, I'm even more determined to continue making a meaningful difference in the lives of others. I love helping others win—it's just part of my DNA.

When you study altruism, you discover that even small, random acts of kindness can go a long way and have a large impact. It could be a sincere compliment, a few words of encouragement or appreciation, volunteering to do something in the community, giving to a charitable donation, or even mentoring someone who seems lost.

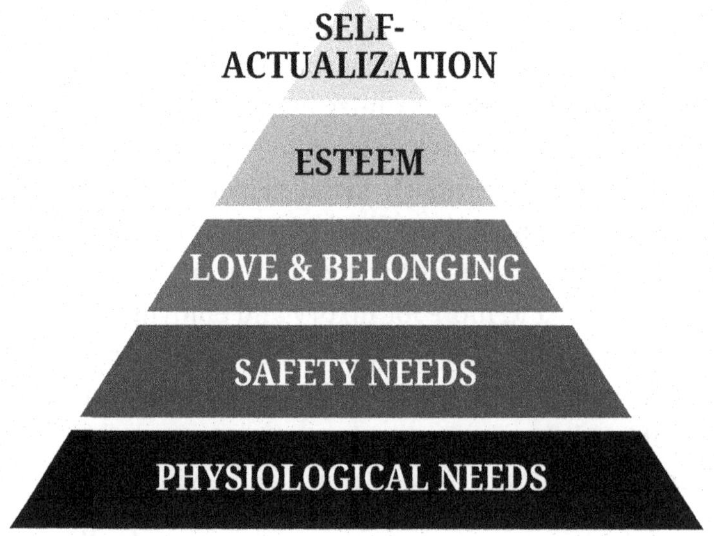

Many years ago, I was introduced to Maslow's Hierarchy of Needs. This theory is summed up with a pyramid (shown above) that shows the different human needs at each level. Basic human needs of life—food, shelter, clothing, and water—are at the bottom; and self-actualization is at the top. Experience has taught me that it's usually easier to help others when all of your own base needs have been met. Helping people meet their needs at each level of Maslow's pyramid can lead to incredible ripple effects throughout society. Lifting just one person positions them closer to the top, making it easier for them to help the next person.

Quadrant 3 is when we are really beginning to be able to pour into others at the highest level, perhaps even as a sage. That's when we have the time, the resources, and the decades of experience to enable us to help others think and do life better. (Actually, this particular benefit is one that might overlay into both Quadrant 3 and Quadrant 4.)

Another big factor in achieving personal fulfilment is building a strong community and support system. We have the power to choose who we allow to stay in our lives and who we choose to invest time with. This is extremely important, as you become your community.

Throughout history, many of the world's great leaders knew one another, even if they were in different industries. One of the greatest illustrations of this is Bill Gates and his long-term friendship with Warren Buffett. ("As iron sharpens iron, so a man sharpens the countenance of his friend" [Proverbs 27:17].) In the same way, we can be intentional about carefully choosing our friends, who we work for and with, and who becomes our clients and customers. Who we hang out with will influence us; they will inspire both our thinking and our attitude, and thereby either lift us up or push us down. Much of our legacy, then, is determined by who we choose to put into our community.

Perhaps the most important decision we make is choosing the person to whom we make a lifelong commitment. I believe when you marry a person, you marry into a family. As I mentioned in the introduction, we were very blessed that our daughters both chose to marry quality young men, and we are also blessed that they both come from extraordinary families. It's not about perfection, because everyone is going to make mistakes; it's simply about being smart about who you hang with because they will slowly define your lifestyle—and your legacy.

Another component of personal fulfilment is the joy that comes with celebrating successes and milestones. A great life is one where you make people smile, you encourage them, you love them, and you appreciate them. I constantly think ahead and search for ways to cheer others on, regardless of whether they're a valet, a house cleaner, or waitstaff. And that certainly applied to my kids as well, as I became the president of their fan club. I wanted to be the parent who poured energy into them, cheered them on, loved them, and was transparent and intentional with them more than any other parent; and the results have been amazing. We have two incredible adult daughters!

Health and Wellness

Positioning yourself for this Reaping Quadrant, of course, means not only being efficient with your money management; it also involves preserving your health by being specific with your efforts in that arena. Some people don't play out their energy toward sustaining their health as much as they should in the first two quadrants—and I was among them! When I crossed the fifty-year mark, though, something happened to make me realize I had failed to create the health habits I could have. My parents were incredible, and they left me such a powerful legacy with giant parental privilege; yet it was void of helping me understand how the body worked. Unfortunately, my mom even died obese.

Then when I was fifty I had a chance encounter with a friend who had made a drastic change in his life. I had not seen him for a while, and at a breakfast meeting with him one morning he explained that his dramatic weight loss had occurred because he came to understand that a big part of health is all about what you eat. As is the case with a lot of people, I knew that; yet I had not really taken it to heart. I was overweight; and when I looked at myself in the mirror shortly after that, I recognized I was not modeling good health practices or leaving a proper legacy in that area for my family—so I changed. For the next multiple years, I put heavy interest and emphasis on learning how the body works, traveling and meeting with some of the best doctors in the world, studying the body, and writing books on the subject.

Telling that part of my legacy in my books is impacting thousands of others, and that is very rewarding to me. The books I love to give away most are *Strategic Parenting*, which tells the 100 things my wife and I did to raise extraordinary kids, and my four books on health. In fact, I created an entire health bar in my RESULTS Center where I keep these books to give to people who come there, because those are the life areas where I want to have the biggest impact. Yes, I love to teach them how to make more money and grow their businesses; yet I want even more to be able to pattern interrupt people who come into my life and get them on the track of pouring into their kids and grandkids and into their own health, so they too can leave a great legacy.

Prioritizing your physical health is one of the most important aspects of leaving a great legacy. If you are unhealthy, both your personal and business lives can suffer since you're not as strong as you need to be mentally or physically to multitask and operate with excellence in either area.

It's the healthy habits you create that make the difference. Decades of research show that exercise, eating healthy, and maintaining proper weight are the three most important habits you can adopt to enhance longevity.

Obviously, physical exercise matters; and it should be regular, frequent, and ongoing. Strength resistance, cardiovascular exercise (aerobics), balance, and stretching all promote a better-operating body. In fact, daily exercise can turn back the hands of time. Just thirty minutes of sustained activity most days of the week can literally change or even save your life! If you can add thirty minutes of movement to your day, you will transform your health! On the other hand, studies have proven that a lack of cardiovascular fitness through regular exercise is linked with high blood pressure, obesity, diabetes, heart disease, and strokes, in addition to increased stress, cancer, and other disease states that shorten life. The science is there. Exercise heals.

You truly are what you eat. People eat for two basic reasons—hunger and appetite. Hunger is the need for food—a physical reaction that includes chemical changes in your body, It's an instinctive, protective mechanism that ensures your body gets the fuel it requires to function reasonably well. On the other hand, appetite is simply the desire for food. It's a sensory reaction that stimulates an involuntary physiological response—a conditioned response to food.

The healthy thing to do, then, is to eat to live, not live to eat. The primary task of nutrition is to figure out which foods provide the energy and building material you need to construct and maintain every organ and system in your body. A proper nutrition management includes controlling your calory and carbohydrate intake, choosing the right time to eat, breaking the sugar habit, and staying sufficiently hydrated.

As necessary as exercise and proper nutrition are, they are not the whole picture. There is one more piece to the wellness puzzle, and that is getting regular health screenings and checkups. Early detection of an illness can save your life, so it's important to stay current on screenings, bloodwork reviews, EKGs, MRIs, hormone testing, urinalysis, mammograms, and any other pertinent preventive tests. Create a medical support team that includes doctors, nutritionists, dieticians, and anyone else who has a professional understanding of your body and can help you assess, quantify, and monitor progress on a scientific level. Knowledge is power!

Of course, your mental health can also have a big impact on your physical health. You may want to ask yourself these questions: *Am I managing anxiety and making a conscious effort to eliminate stress. Is my life aligned with my values? Have I set up harmony in my home, office, and life so things run as smoothy as possible? Is my pace of life contributing to or detracting from my overall well-being?*

One of the major causes of disease, aging, and death is stress. Stress occurs when your mental, physical, or spiritual challenges exceed your ability to cope with them. **Stress kills**—literally. It causes your body to secrete hormones (cortisol and adrenaline) that can have a negative impact on your health.

It's not just important to simply manage stress; rather, it's vital that you virtually eliminate it from your life. Reduced stress will improve your business life, your relationships, and your physical well-being. Stress can be situational and caused by several factors, including how you plan, react to, and cope with what you allow in your life.

There will always be obstacles and issues in life that are outside your control. Stress is what happens when pressure builds in the gap between the things we want to do and the things we are actually doing. It often results from a lack of congruence between the life you want—your goals—and the life you live. For instance, if your goal is to live a debt-free life and yet you have mountains of credit-card bills rolling in, you will experience stress as a consequence. If you are constantly rushing around and always late for meetings, kids' sports activities, or church, you are creating stress during the process of getting to and from events instead of enjoying the journey.

The best way to cure stress is to drill down to the source of the problem and cut stress out before it even happens. If you do a "life audit" and make a list of the top ten most stressful things that happen on a daily basis, you will begin to discover a lot of habits and processes—or lack thereof—that could be modified. By changing certain habits, you can eliminate most sources of stress in your life. It's important that you simplify your life, which will inevitably lead to a lot less stress. Your true wealth is determined by the amount of things you don't have to worry about. Worry is a stressor.

Note: The stress-related impact on your health is not always readily apparent. Sometimes it takes years or even decades before you feel the consequences of stress. The compound effect of negative influences add up each day.

It's important to pay attention to your stress level, which affects your mental health, and seek professional help when you need it. Having said that, there are many stress-management techniques you can implement that will reduce or even eliminate stress in your life. Let's look at four:

1. Time management. Often the most frequent stressor in your life is a lack of time. If you drill down to the core of many of your stress issues, you'll see that a lack of time is not actually

producing the stress; the cause of the stress is ineffective time management.

Building margin time into your life is one of the fastest ways to eliminate stress. Margin time also allows you to make room for life's unexpected events. When you have extra time, you can accept an interruption with grace, talk to an old friend who calls at the last minute, or help someone in need. Without built-in margin time, you will feel pressed and stressed.

2. Removing toxins. Toxins are pervasive in our environment and in our bodies and can be linked to just about every chronic and autoimmune disease. Your detoxification system encompasses the liver, kidneys, intestines, and skin, and to a lesser extent all the other tissues. Your body is designed to filter out toxins, and yet you can put yourself at an advantage if you avoid toxins altogether. Some of the ways you can do that include eating organic; choosing all-natural, biodegradable cleaning products; getting plenty of fresh air; choosing skincare products that are as close to nature as possible; making sure you drink clean water, and cooking with healthier oils.
3. Choosing who you invest your time with. If you are hanging around people who always seem to have a negative opinion about things and are generally critical, you probably need to make some changes. Your stress level will be immediately enhanced when you start being around people who lift you up and encourage you to reach your goals and dreams—who inspire you to reach higher levels.
4. Managing your money. If you overspend, you will have stress—period. By not managing your cashflow, you are

accepting a life where other people will determine your circumstances.

Of course, money itself doesn't make you happier. It cannot buy everything, and yet it can definitely help support many of the things in life that are important. Money is a tool to achieve your independence and to allow your children to build a financially sound future. Having money makes life less risky and in many cases less stressful. If you are sick, you can afford the best doctors. If you want to invest, you can afford to invest without affecting your lifestyle. When you have money, you can send your kids to the best schools, and you can travel or spend money on entertainment as you desire. You can give to your church and help others, as you're led. Certainly living life well—and with less stress—includes elevating the importance of faith, family, and friends, and those things need to be a huge part of your focus. Making money should never supersede those things; rather, it should support them.

Quadrant 3, the Reaping Quadrant, can and should be one of the most fulfilling times of your life. Yet if you apply these principles that enable you to create financial security and live a healthy life, you will be even more fulfilled in Quadrant 4, the Returning Quadrant.

CHAPTER THREE READER RESPONSE

For those who are currently in this quadrant:

1. Name 3 to 5 things that matter most to you at this stage of your life and the conscious actions you are taking toward each.

    1. ____

    ____

    ____

    2. ____

    ____

    ____

    3. ____

    ____

    ____

    4. ____

    ____

    ____

    5. ____

    ____

    ____

2. Describe how you are reaping rewards from the things you have achieved in your life to this point:

 ____

 ____

 ____

 ____

3. Can you truly say of your most recent year, "*This was the best year ever because I've become a better person, I've become more impactful, and I've experienced an incredible year*"? If not, why not, and how can you make that statement apply to your current year?

 ____

 ____

 ____

 ____

4. On a scale of 1 to 5, with 5 being the highest, how diligent have you been in building a legacy for your kids and others who are watching how you earn, save, and invest money, and how you've spent it in relationship to how much you make? ______ If you rated yourself less than 5, what can you do to improve your rating during this quadrant of your life?

 ____

 ____

 ____

5. What have you intentionally done or what can you do now to position your kids and launch them into the world?

____

____

6. How can you intentionally pour values into your grandchildren?

____

____

7. Name some of your family traditions that lend toward building a legacy:

   1. ____________________________________
   2. ____________________________________
   3. ____________________________________
   4. ____________________________________

8. Have you designed your life to include time to enjoy your home and your family? If not, what changes can you make to allow that pleasure at this point in your life?

____

____

____

9. Do you have a job, a career, or a vocation (everyday work efforts fall into your sweet spot and you love your professional life so much that you literally just want more

of the same)? If your answer was “a job” or “a career,” what passions could you now develop into a vocation, and how?

____

____

____

10. In what ways are you achieving personal fulfillment in this quadrant of your life?

____

____

____

____

11. On a scale of 1 to 5, with 5 being the highest, how well have you done in preserving your health so far? _____ If you rated yourself less than 5, what are you committed to doing to improve your health from this point forward?

____

____

____

CHAPTER THREE VIPS

1. The third quadrant, called Reaping, should encapsulate many wins—like more flexibility of your time and perhaps even more intentional altruism, whereby you are impacting lives to another level while you're enjoying the life you've set up for yourself.
2. Ideally, you've been effective with your finances during your Earning Quadrant, meaning you've been diligent in building a legacy for your kids and others who are watching how you earn, save, and invest money, and how you spend it in relationship to how much you make. If you've done this successfully, you can move into this next quadrant in an optimized position to reap some of the financial security you've built.
3. By the time you cross over into your fifties and move into Quadrant 3, you have had many life experiences, ups and downs, and twists and turns, many of which have made you better and allowed you to navigate more intentionally. Hopefully, you can look back at every day, every week, every month, and every year and be happy that you're reaping the rewards of the many relationships you've built and the life you've set up for yourself.
4. For most people, practicing altruism and giving back plays a huge role in the personal fulfilment you often reap in the third quadrant. The quality of helping others be champions or win more can not only springboard you to success in life; it can also bring you much more fulfilment than you can get from virtually anything else.

5. Positioning yourself for this Reaping Quadrant means not only being efficient with your money management; it also involves preserving your health by being specific with your efforts in that arena. Prioritizing your physical health is one of the most important aspects of leaving a great legacy. It not only models good health habits to your descendants; it also enables you to reap the rewards you've accumulated in previous quadrants and allows you to build a better life for your family and others around you.

CHAPTER FOUR

Quadrant 4—Returning (75–100)

What you leave behind is not
what is engraved in stone monuments,
but what is woven into the lives of others.

Pericles

As you reach Quadrant 4, you're approaching the pinnacle of what has hopefully been a well-lived life. Everything you've done to this point has affected your significance and impact on this world. The generations below you have been shaped by your imprint and the people you've led have been transformed by your guidance. It's in this quadrant that you will solidify your legacy by shifting your focus even more to returning—giving back and sharing the gifts you've been given.

Enjoying Life

This quadrant is not all about giving, of course. With more free time and flexibility, this phase of life can be a great opportunity to pursue new hobbies, enjoy even more travel, and invest more time with loved ones. It's a great time to declutter your life and live more simply. (See my book *Strategic Simplicity*.) Simplicity, in fact, can be a gift at this stage of your life that creates space for things like serving others, reading, investing time with your grandchildren, praying and meditating on God's Word, hobbies, travel, or whatever else is important to you.

It's important to find meaningful and enjoyable ways to fill your time and stay active and engaged during this phase. The more active and intentional you are, the more you have to look forward to. Of course, you will have more time to pursue leisure activities and interests that bring you joy and fulfilment, such as gardening, joining a club, playing a musical instrument, or engaging in sports of all kinds.

Charlie Chaplin died at age 88. He left us four profound statements:

1. Nothing is eternal in this world, not even our problems.
2. I like to walk in the rain because no one can see my tears.
3. The most wasted day in life is the day we don't laugh.
4. The six best doctors in the world:
    a. Sunshine
    b. Rest
    c. Exercise
    d. Diet
    e. Self-esteem
    f. Friends

Keep them in all stages of your life and enjoy a healthy life.

I want to encourage you to continue setting goals, even in this fourth quadrant of your life. Setting goals—at any age—gives you clearly defined objectives to work toward and a focus that keeps you moving forward toward improvement and betterment in the various areas of your life. And that model is truly a double win because others are watching and being impacted by your discipline. Setting goals in this quadrant of your life will help ensure you are continuing to do things you think are important and valuable, and achieving them brings a great deal of satisfaction and reward.

My great friend, partner, and mentor Peter Thomas, who is well into this quadrant and has already accomplished more than probably 99 percent of people in this world, still has more goals than almost anyone I know. He and I meet once or twice a year and do what we call annual summits; we share about experiences, books we've come across, and plan for the months and year ahead. We walk, ride bikes, hike, have coffee and great dinners, and even do super fun things like jet skiing and auto auctions; and we even talk about business deals.

In this stage of your life, I encourage you to set even more goals, update old ones, and team up with others of like mind so you can continue to learn and grow. This may involve exploring new hobbies (like pickleball, perhaps), learning new interests, taking classes or workshops (online or in person)—or even teaching classes—volunteering for community projects, learning and using social media, and certainly staying curious and open to new experiences.

In my book *RESULTSaholic*™ (2024), I talk about the type of people who typically come to our RESULTS Center to supercharge their thinking for turning their visions into reality. They all have a craving for faster results, they are always seeking *Best Practices*, and they fall into the highest category of our RESULTSaholic™ model—what we call the *Optimizer*.

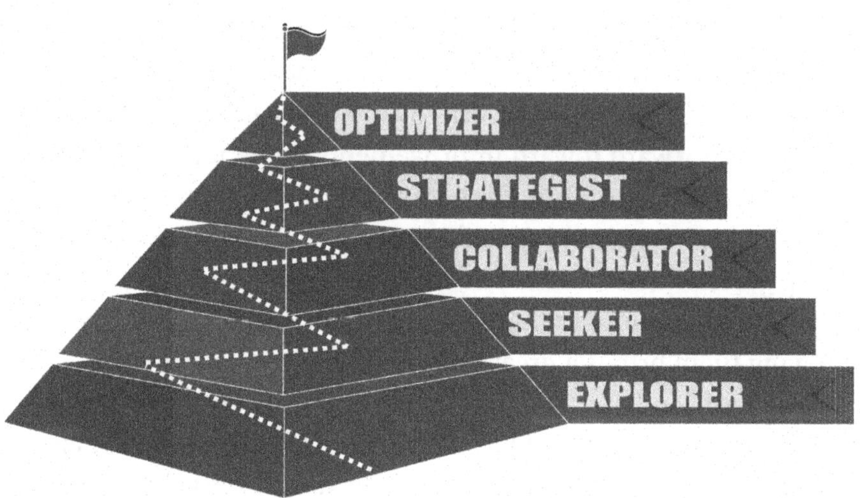

In essence, *Optimizers* continuously evaluate and refine every aspect of their lives, striving for efficiency and effectiveness, and they are loving life and living it to the fullest. Many of you reading this book likely fall into this category, and there's no reason that has to change as you progress in age. By continuing to set and achieve goals, you can still find extreme fulfillment every day of your life.

We can learn a ton about living highly successfully in this quadrant—or any other, for that matter—from a favorite book of mine called *Enjoy the Ride* by Steve Gilliland. The book serves as a guide for finding more joy, hope, and purpose in life, ultimately empowering readers to make the most of their journey, embrace their unique path, and find joy in the present moment. The book is structured around three central themes:

1. Personal Responsibility: It's important to take responsibility for your own happiness and success, rather than blaming others or external circumstances. Adopt a proactive mindset and embrace change as a means of personal growth.

2. Positive Thinking: There is power in positive thinking and the influence it has on your life. There are countless examples of individuals who have overcome adversity and achieved their goals by adopting an optimistic outlook and believing in their own abilities.
3. **Enjoying the Journey:** There is great significance in savoring life's journey rather than focusing solely on the destination. True happiness comes from appreciating the present moment and finding pleasure in everyday experiences.

A big part of enjoying the journey in this quadrant certainly includes maintaining and strengthening relationships with friends and loved ones. It's most often a double win, as it can help promote a sense of purpose and belonging and it can be a series of give-back moments. This could include investing time with family or it may involve reconnecting with old friends; the list can be long. Something that could be a win for your family is to start having family meetings to discuss goals or make plans for family events. You could also initiate gatherings of friends or like-minded individuals and facilitate worthwhile discussions.

A meaningful way to gain perspective and appreciate all you have achieved up to this point in life is reflecting on your life experiences and accomplishments with gratitude and appreciation. This may take the form of creating videos, creating old-fashioned photo albums or electronic scrapbooks, simply taking time to reflect on your life journey and the lessons you've learned along the way, or even writing a memoir.

You may even want to do something I talked about in my book *Reflections on Results*, and that is to list as many of the books you can think of that you've read over your lifetime and rate them in the order of the magnitude of impact they've had on your life. In the process, think about how you have changed over the years—how your thinking changed, how your goals changed, and how you became the person you are today. Who were the people who effected that change the most? How different are the results in the various aspects of your life than you thought they would be in your first quadrant of life, and why?

Giving Back

We make a living by what we get,
but we make a life by what we give."
Winston Churchill

As you're considering these questions, ask also how you may bring about even more positive change for others at this stage of your life. Remember, your guidance can make a profound impact on the lives of others and create a lasting legacy of support and inspiration. I coauthored a book called *Advice Matters* with my longtime friend and business mentor, Jay Rodgers. Jay thrives in this quadrant of his life by giving back through a non-profit he founded called Biz Owners Ed, which is devoted to mentoring growing entrepreneurs. You may want to check out this powerful book, which clearly articulates a "wow" model on obtaining the right advice for you.

You could also reciprocate for what you've been given in life by serving on advisory boards and offering your expertise and experience to organizations and businesses in your area. Your insights and guidance could potentially help shape the direction of these entities and create a lasting impact on their success.

One very effective effort that would reach a wider audience would be something we've already lightly mentioned—to share your life lessons and insights by writing a book, or even by creating a blog or a podcast or writing articles for newspapers or magazines. Sharing stories and wisdom from your life could be particularly impactful for and even strengthen bonds with your family members. Your lived experiences can provide invaluable lessons for future generations and create a legacy of love and connection.

Your wisdom could also serve to provide guidance and inspiration for others navigating their own life journeys. I mentioned my good friend Peter Thomas earlier. Peter has been a mentor to numerous young entrepreneurs, family members and friends for many years. Yet in order to share his knowledge to a greater audience, even in his mid-80s, Peter has developed the "One Minute Mentor" for social media platforms.

Peter Thomas' "One-Minute Mentor," December 31, 2024

Three Life-Changing Tips before the New Year: First of all, there's an old Chinese saying, "May you live in interesting times." The next three months, the next twelve months are going to be very interesting times—chaotic, probably disruptive; and in any type of disruption, there are tons of opportunity. That's one thing that's ahead of us. They say that knowledge is knowing the right questions to ask, but wisdom is knowing the right answers. So make this year a year of wisdom. The last thing I want to tell you is live in day-tight compartments. Today is the most important day of your life.

> Yesterday is gone and tomorrow is not here yet, so today is the day you're going to make a difference in the world. Each day, live fully. Happy New Year. 2025, here we come. Be well.

Of course, a highly effective way to give back is through philanthropy and charitable giving. By donating your money and time to causes that resonate with you, you can make a positive impact on the world. Your generosity may not just create lasting change; it could inspire others to give back as well.

Let me throw in a bit of advice here. I suggest that early in the fourth quadrant of your life you start sharing your assets with your family, rather than waiting until you die. Let them enjoy some of your financial resources, jewelry, and other assets while you're still alive and can savor the joy and fulfillment of seeing that happen! I gave my son-in-law a diamond horseshoe ring my dad had. It's probably not worth more than $2,000, but my son-in-law wears it proudly every day! On the other hand, my mom's jewelry sat in a safe until she died; so I never had the opportunity to find out the history behind each piece, and she was robbed of the joy of seeing the ladies in my family wearing them.

Now, granted, most kids today are not interested in many of the things that we as adults value. Typically, they care nothing about the expensive furniture or dinnerware that we have put so much stock in over the years. I asked some of the younger people on my team what they would value being given by their parents. One said real estate, and another said their stories. So something I probably need to address with my kids is whether they want to inherit our condo and keep it as a family lake home, or if they would prefer to sell it and get the cash. As for the family stories, we'll talk more about that in part 2 of this book.

Overall, the Returning Quadrant is a time for reflection, leisure, continued personal growth, and giving back to society. By focusing on these key areas, you can make the most of this phase of life and find fulfilment and joy in all you have accomplished. In fact, this should be a time when you position yourself to enjoy the life you live every day.

I encourage you to prioritizing your own well-being and personal growth through practicing and modeling self-care as you move into this quadrant. Maintaining a healthy mind, body, and spirit allows you to continue making meaningful contributions to the world and enjoying a fulfilling life.

You can prepare even more intentionally to leave a powerful legacy through the process of meaningful communication—specifically, in the act of writing letters and creating videos about the things that matter. In part 2, we show you how your well-thought-out words can be instruments of blessing and forever impact the generations beneath you.

CHAPTER FOUR READER RESPONSE

1. What new hobbies and leisure activities are you pursuing or do you want to pursue at this stage of your life?

   ____

   ____

2. What are your current goals in each of the following areas:

   To Have: ________________________________

   ____

   To Share: ________________________________

   ____

   To Give: ________________________________

   ____

   To Experience: ____________________________

   ____

   To Become: ______________________________

   ____

3. On what level do you think you fit on the RESULTSaholoc™ model, and why?

   ____

   ____

4. On a scale of 1 to 5, with 5 being the highest, how much do you think you are "enjoying the ride" in each of these three areas? If less than five, list one or two ways you can move to the highest level.

   1. Personal responsibility: Rating:_____ Ways to improve:

      ____

      ____

   2. Positive thinking: Rating: _____ Ways to improve:

      ____

      ____

   3. Enjoying the journey: Rating: _____ Ways to improve:

      ____

      ____

5. On a scale of 1 to 5, with 5 being the highest, how successful have you been in preserving special life experiences and accomplishments in the form of videos, scrapbooks, etc.? _____ If you rated yourself less than five, name what you can invest time in doing to preserve these while you still have time on this earth:

   ____

   ____

   ____

   ____

6. How are you bringing about positive change for others at this stage of your life?

___

___

___

7. Have you considered writing a book, creating a blog or a podcast, or writing articles for newspapers or magazines to share stories and wisdom from your life? Which of these would you like to do, and what are some intentional actions you can take to move you forward? (Consider reaching out to us to help you write a book, if that is one of your choices.)

___

___

___

8. Seriously consider becoming a mentor for one or more individuals as a way to give back during this quadrant of your life.
9. In what ways do you give back through philanthropy and charitable giving?

___

___

___

10. Have you begun sharing your assets with your family now, versus having them wait until you die to enjoy them?

11. On a scale of 1 to 5, with 5 being the highest, how well are you practicing and modeling self-care as you move into this quadrant as it relates to maintaining a healthy mind, body, and spirit? _____ If you rated less than a five, what steps can you take to improve?

____

____

____

CHAPTER FOUR VIPS

1. It's in Quadrant 4 that you will solidify your legacy by shifting your focus even more to returning—giving back and sharing the gifts you've been given.
2. With more free time and flexibility, this phase of life can be a great opportunity to pursue new hobbies, enjoy even more travel, and invest more time with loved ones.
3. It's important to continue setting goals, even in this fourth quadrant of your life. Setting goals—at any age—gives you clearly defined objectives to work toward and a focus that keeps you moving forward toward improvement and betterment in the various areas of your life.
4. We can learn a ton about living highly successfully in this quadrant—or any other, for that matter—from a book called *Enjoy the Ride* by Steve Gilliland. The book serves as a guide for finding more joy, hope, and purpose in life, ultimately empowering readers to make the most of their journey, embrace their unique path, and find joy in the present moment.
5. A meaningful way to gain perspective and appreciate all you have achieved up to this point in life is reflecting on your life experiences and accomplishments with gratitude and appreciation.
6. Ask how you may bring about even more positive change in the lives of others at this stage of your life. Remember, your guidance can make a profound impact on the lives of others and create a lasting legacy of support and inspiration. This

could come in the form of mentoring those in the younger generation, serving on advisory boards, writing a book or creating a blog or podcast, or philanthropy and charitable giving.

PART TWO

Impart a Legacy of Love through the Power of Blessing

Note from Greg Vaughn: Part two of this book is based on my twenty years of teaching the *Letters from Dad* program to tens of thousands of men all around the globe. What I experienced, though, was that many of the women started saying to me, "Hey, what about us? When are you going to do something for us?" So I also created a video series for women called *Blessings from the Heart*. In this book, I'm bringing those two programs together and speaking to both men and women. It's generic, because what I taught to men is applicable for women as well. In fact, I learned that letter writing generally comes much more naturally for women than it does for men.

Let me just briefly speak to something else here: I'm a follower of Christ. I have spoken to millions of people, both on secular radio and to diverse groups; and within my audience there may be atheists, there may be Muslims, or there may be Hindus. It doesn't matter. The message I bring is simply this: At the end of life, and even in the middle of life, don't you think it would be a good idea to speak words of encouragement and blessing and to put that in writing, no matter who you are and what you believe? Can we agree on that? If so, then just simply understand that I may come at it in a different way than you do, but that's who I am. Please interpret these teachings I'm giving you through your own belief system.

Please view Video Intro:

CHAPTER FIVE

The Power of the Written Word

A Story to Inspire:

What an honor it is for me to take you on this wonderful journey. I cannot tell you the joy I've experienced as I've discovered the power of the written word in my own family.

I was leading a legacy group one evening in Dallas, and a young man expressed his excitement about writing a letter to his soon-to-be born first child to welcome him into the world. When he said that, I realized I had missed an opportunity to do that with my first grandson. When my grandson was two months old, I sat down and crafted a letter to him describing my thoughts and feelings as I went into the hospital room to meet him for the first time. After writing the letter, I thought I should wait a while, until he was old enough to appreciate it; so I stuffed it where every man stuffs their important treasures in life—in my underwear drawer.

Frankly, I forgot about the letter. Fast forward to eight years later. My grandson was staying at our home for the weekend, and it was always my tradition to read him a quick Bible story before he went to bed. So afterward, when I kissed him and put him to bed, I was walking out of the room when I suddenly remembered the letter I had written many years before. I said, 'Oh my goodness, son, I have something for you. I'll be right back." I went into my bedroom and found the letter I had written to him when he was two months old. I handed the letter to him, and he opened it carefully. When he saw the date, his eyes got big; and he said, "Papa, I don't want to read it. I want you to read it so I can listen more carefully to the words."

I won't quote that letter to you because it's a little long, but please allow me to paraphrase what I communicated:

> Son, I'll never forget being in the hospital room when they brought you to see me. There were sixteen people in the room. I didn't even have the opportunity to hold you that day, and I felt like the odd man out. I must confess, as I leaned up against the wall, I thought to myself, *I know I'm supposed to be excited; but frankly, it really isn't the kind of excitement I expected.* But two months later, something special happened. We got to keep you overnight. At two o'clock in the morning, I heard all kinds of commotion going on in the living room. I walked in to see an exhausted grandmother trying to give you a bottle.
>
> I'll never forget it. I said to your grandmother, "Let me have the bottle. I'll give it to him." She said, "Do you even remember how to do this?" I said, "How many kids have I raised?" She gave me the bottle. I remember looking into your eyes and you looked into mine, and something magical happened in my spirit that I'll never forget. You became mine. I remember placing my hand on your little head and praying a blessing over your life. I prayed that you would come to know Christ at an early age and that you would serve Him all the days of your life.

At that point, my grandson jumped to his feet, threw his arms in the air, and said, "Papa! God answered that prayer! I did come to know Jesus at an early age, and I do love him with all my heart." As I finished the letter, he handed it back to me and said, "Papa, will you keep this letter safe for me because I'm afraid I might lose it?"

It is that kind of joyous experience I believe you can have in your life as you write and learn to bless those who are special in your life.

For the last forty years, I've had the honor of heading up the film production side of the company I founded called Grace Ministries. When this *Letters from Dad* ministry came into my life, I placed the video ministry in the capable hands of my son David and hit the road. I watched God do a miracle as we launched *Letters from Dad* in over 3,000 churches. But frankly, after about ten years on the road, I was worn out. My wife and family suggested it was time to give it a rest and simply trust God for the future of the *Letters from Dad* ministry. So, I jumped back into the film production side and began producing what I thought were some very-much-needed resources for the church.

I produced what I call the *101 Series*. These were video series, like *Marriage 101*, *Back to the Basics—Family 101*, and *Crisis 101*. However, there was one subject—reconciliation—that I really wanted to address, but I couldn't get clarification on how to do it. That is, until I was preparing "The Power of the Written Word," in the *Lessons from the Tackle Box*, the updated version of the *Letters from Dad* program. That's when I realized this series could really be subtitled "Reconciliation 101, Back to the Basics."

I don't care how good you are, there'll be times in your life you get turned upside down with your wife, your child(ren), your teenagers, or maybe with your parents, your pastor, or your boss. I'm telling you; it's going to happen. It is my prayer that through our journey together, you'll learn some new skills that will help you through these difficult times.

Over and over, I've seen marriages and families restored. One man said, "I was living upstairs, and she was living downstairs, and we weren't even communicating except through our kids. And believe me, that's sick. Then God did a miracle through the power of the written word. A simple letter slipped under her door, and it changed our life forever."

I've seen great marriages made better. I'll never forget the letter from a lady in California. She said, "I never thought you could teach an old dog new tricks, but you have. My husband hasn't written to me in fifty years, but on Mother's Day he handed me a framed letter. I am so blessed because of that letter, and he read it out loud in front of our large family."

I've seen fathers reunited with the children they have been estranged from, and I've seen men who have not spoken to their parents in years come back together with them. One man wrote: "Dear Greg, you once asked the men in our group, 'What is the one thing you would ask God to do in your *Letters from Dad* experience?' The answer to that question for me was to restore the fractured relationship with my mother. We had not spoken in five years; and I knew I had to reach out to her, so I wrote her a letter of blessing. I placed it in a beautiful treasure box; and for some reason, I felt compelled to send it overnight by Federal Express. God had directed my thoughts in doing so because it arrived on my mom's birthday, which I had forgotten. When she opened the box and read my letter, she immediately called; and we spent over an hour on the phone with lots of tears and emotions. God did a miracle and restored my relationship with my mom, and I know it would not have happened unless I had acted on the things I had learned through *Letters from Dad*."

Reconciliation. What does that word even mean? Well, Webster's Dictionary says it means "to make right with those you're in conflict with, to restore friendly relationships, to enable or bring about peace, to resolve differences, or to live together in harmony."

For those of us who follow Christ, the most important reconciliation story of all time is the reconciliation of God to man that is recorded for us in the written words of the Bible. (See Romans 5:10, Colossians 1:19-20, and 2 Corinthians 5:17-19). No matter what you believe, you can pursue reconciliation in your home with your wife, your children, your parents, or your brothers or sisters; with your coworkers; or with anyone else with whom you've had a broken relationship.

One of the most painful things in my life was being in conflict with my best friend in the world, my oldest brother. My brother and I had been best friends forever. We lived together until we were twenty-five years old, and then we married. There had hardly been a day in our lives when we hadn't spoken together by phone. That is, until my mom became extremely ill, and she asked me to serve as the executor of her estate. When she died, I was thrust into conflict with parts of my family; and that broke off my relationship and my communication with my brother. It was a terrible few years; and during those years, I found that my words failed. No matter what I said, I just made matters worse. Have you ever been in that situation? It's not a fun place to be, is it? It was when I wrote a simple letter to my brother that I think the ice began to thaw. I tried to communicate my sorrow and my sadness for all that had led to our broken relationship. Frankly, I don't remember exactly what I said; but God in his mercy restored that relationship.

May I ask you a question? Who are you in conflict with today? Maybe it's one person, or maybe it's multiple people. I suggest you begin praying or thinking about what your next step may be that you can take in humility to restore this relationship.

It may just be that you need to write a letter to someone. I'm going to help you write one; it's called the "I am Blessed" letter. It's easy to write, and I believe you'll enjoy writing it. And here's a unique tweak: I suggest you frame the letter and deliver it to someone special in your life.

I wrote the "I am Blessed" letter to my wife, Carolyn, and it hangs just to the left of where she spends a good amount of her time fixing her hair and putting on her makeup every day.

As you read my letter to my wife, I suggest you take your pen and circle anything that applies to your spouse or to whomever you're going to write.

My Dearest Carolyn,

Today, I want to give you a blessing.

I'm blessed to have you, my dear and loving wife.

I'm blessed because you love the Lord Jesus Christ.

I'm blessed because you are a prayer warrior on my behalf.

I'm blessed because you forgive me when I act in a sinful manner.

I'm blessed because you have modeled what real love is to me.

I'm blessed because you always give me wise counsel.

I'm blessed because you have a tender heart and a loving spirit.

I am blessed because you chose me to be your life partner.

I'm blessed because you always speak to me in an honoring manner.

I'm blessed because God gave you a tender heart to love our children.

I'm blessed to experience your music, smile,
and contagious laughter.
I am forever blessed because we get to spend eternity together.
God never allows lives to meet without a reason; and
because of you, my life will never be the same, for you'll
always be my dear friend and loving wife.
Blessings to you now and forever,
Gregory

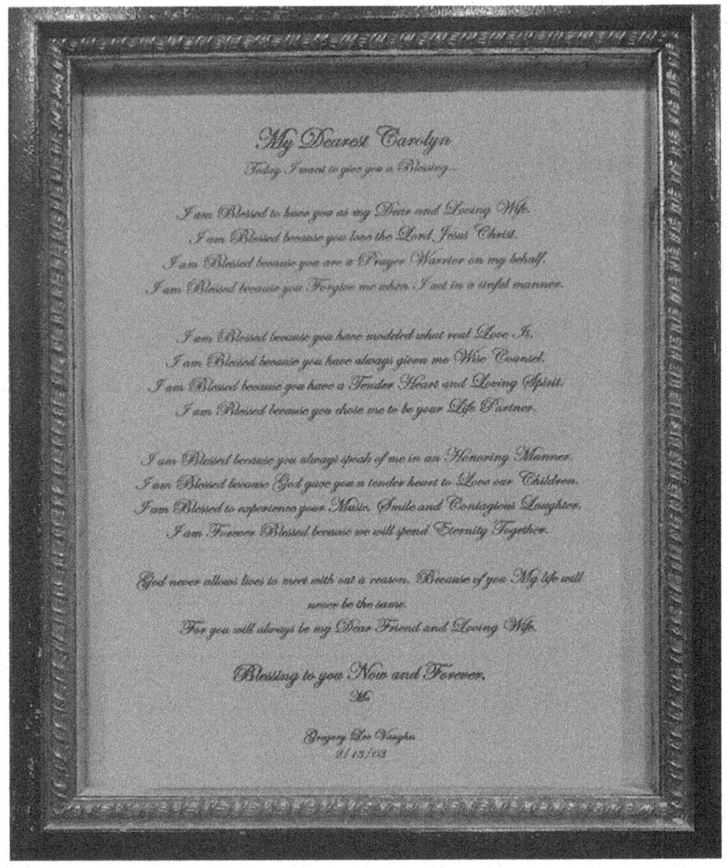

My Dearest Carolyn
Today I want to give you a Blessing...

I am Blessed to have you as my Dear and Loving Wife.
I am Blessed because you love the Lord Jesus Christ.
I am Blessed because you are a Prayer Warrior on my behalf.
I am Blessed because you Forgive me when I act in a sinful manner.

I am Blessed because you have modeled what real Love Is.
I am Blessed because you have always given me Wise Counsel.
I am Blessed because you have a Tender Heart and Loving Spirit.
I am Blessed because you chose me to be your Life Partner.

I am Blessed because you always speak of me in an Honoring Manner.
I am Blessed because God gave you a tender heart to Love our Children.
I am Blessed to experience your Music, Smile and Contagious Laughter.
I am Forever Blessed because we will spend Eternity Together.

God never allows lives to meet with out a reason. Because of you My life will never be the same.
For you will always be my Dear Friend and Loving Wife.

Blessing to you Now and Forever,
Me

Gregory Lee Vaughn
2/13/03

I hope as you read the letter, it gave you a feel and flavor for the kind of words you want to present in your letter so you can just begin filling in the blanks with why you're blessed to have this person in your life.

"I am Blessed Because..." Form Letter

This is the most versatile blessing letter written in *Letters from Dad*. Fill in the blanks and then transfer to your stationary or paper. Present your letter on a special occasion in an attractive frame.

Dear ____________________

On this ____________________, I want to give you a Blessing.

I am Blessed because ____________________________________.

I am Blessed because ____________________________________.

I am Blessed because ____________________________________.

I am Blessed because ____________________________________.

I am Blessed because ____________________________________.

I am Blessed because ____________________________________.

I am Blessed because ____________________________________.

I am Blessed because ____________________________________.

I am Blessed because ____________________________________.

I am Blessed because ____________________________________.

I am Blessed because ____________________________________.

I am Blessed because ____________________________________.

My life is richer and has greater joy because of you.

____ (your full name)

_____________________________ (date)

So, who's going to receive your letter? If you're married, I want to encourage you to write to your spouse; but if you're not married, write to your mom, your dad, your niece, your nephew, or someone else you love. The options are unlimited.

I'd like to share a story of how this powerful letter has been used. My dear friend Steve Sweeney was ministering to his best friend Lee, who was dying of cancer. It was two days before Mother's Day, and he knew Lee would not be able to get a card for his wife. So Steve took the letter I just read and said to Lee, "I'm going to read this, and you tell me what applies so I can write a letter on your behalf that you can give to your wife for Mother's Day." As he read my letter, his friend lifted his oxygen mask and said, "Steve, everything applies; but add this: 'Thank you for being such a great caretaker to me.'" Steve wrote the letter for his friend and had it framed, wrapped, and ready for him to deliver to his wife Terri on Mother's Day.

Terri later told Steve what happened:

> I walked into the hospital room like I do every day, and Lee had a big smile on his face, like he's always had. But I thought, *Okay, this is an even bigger smile.* He couldn't contain himself, and he told me to look over to the couch area. I did and said, "What is this?" It was a present that was beautifully wrapped, and he said, "Do you know what today is?" And I said, "I do not. All I know is I'm here. You're my day. You're my joy every day." Then I said, "Should I stick my hand in it? Is it going to bite me?" He said, "No, Terri." So I opened it, and

> it was a pretty framed letter. He asked again, "Do you know what day it is?" I said, "I do not, and I feel bad because you're my joy. You're my life. I think of you every day." He just said, "It's Mother's Day, and it's a letter I wrote. I couldn't write it myself, but it came from the heart. Our friend Steve helped me with it." I read it, and it was a very lovely piece of his heart that he had always given me and my son for thirty-plus years; it was a joyful day that day. But this letter is going to be more meaningful, and I will treasure it forever because two weeks after Mother's Day, he passed away. This letter is going to be a treasure for the rest of my life.

I'm confident the letters you write will be as joyful and meaningful and will be a treasure to your loved ones as well. Do you think there is any amount of money Lee's wife Terri would take for that treasure—the letter her husband wrote and framed for her? One day you'll be gone from this Earth, and this framed letter you will be writing will be like a stone of remembrance to someone special in your life.

I pray that blessings will be upon you as you write your letter and let someone know why you are blessed to have them in your life.

Let's look now at "The Power of the Spoken Blessing."

P.S: You may ask: "Is it worth taking the time and effort to write the ones you love and cherish?" Here's your answer: At the beginning of this chapter, I shared with you about writing to my first grandson, Hayden, when he was two months old. As I was writing this chapter in the book, my phone beeped. It was a text from my now twenty-two-year-old Hayden. Here is what he said:

Hi Papa,

Things are going well away at college; but today I needed some encouragement, so I read and reread some of the written words you have sent me through the years. I will be eternally grateful for your written words to me. I would like to remind you to keep on writing to the other grandchildren in our big family.

These words are the treasure of my life. Keep on writing, Papa.

Love you,

Hayden

CHAPTER FIVE READER RESPONSE

- Choose the person you want to receive the "I am Blessed" letter.
- Review the template you see in this chapter. Copy it onto your own practice paper, or you can write directly in the book if you wish.
- Begin filling in the blanks with the thoughts of how that person has blessed your life.
- Once you have completed the list, you can transfer all you have written to some nice letterhead paper. I strongly suggest you put it in your handwriting, even if it's not that good. It's more personal and will have a greater effect. If that seems overwhelming, at least add a couple of sentences in your own hand as a P.S. at the end.
- Frame it and pick the date, time, and place for delivery. I guarantee it will be a treasured time of remembrance for that special person in your life.

CHAPTER FIVE VIPS

1. Reconciliation means "to make right with those you're in conflict with, to restore friendly relationships, to enable or bring about peace, to resolve differences, or to live together in harmony." No matter what you believe, you can pursue reconciliation in your home with your wife, your children, your parents, or your brothers or sisters; with your coworkers; or with anyone else with whom you've had a broken relationship.
2. No matter who you are in conflict with, whether it's one person or multiple people, you may need to write an "I Am Blessed" letter to someone. If you're married, you may want to write to your spouse; but if you're not married, you may want to write to your mom, your dad, your niece, your nephew, or someone else you love. The options are unlimited.

CHAPTER SIX

The Power of the Spoken Blessing

A Story to Inspire:

This chapter is about the power of the spoken blessing—what it is, and how we give it. The letter we'll be writing in this chapter is called the "I Remember When" letter. Let me assure you, this is a fun letter to write.

I'll begin with a story told by my friend Bodie Spangler about his wonderful childhood memory. (I've taken the liberty of editing and shortening it some for this book.)

> One of my very special memories is of a time after one of my baseball games at the Little League Park. I had gone across the street to watch the high school kids play. I would often go over and just hang on the fence and watch them play and just soak it in. I couldn't wait to grow up to be seventeen or eighteen, when I would be able to hit a ball that far and throw a ball that hard. That particular night, my dad was down the fence not far from me, maybe about ten feet or so; and his friend Martin walked up to him. It must have been a

> while since they had seen each other, because they hugged. After they exchanged greetings and asked how each other was doing, Martin asked, "How are Bodie and Claire?" (I guess he hadn't seen me, even though I was just a few feet away.) I'll never forget what my father said: "Bodie and Claire are doing great. They are such a joy to their mother and me, and we are so pleased with them." I'm 48, and I still get choked up when I remember that; I was hanging on that fence and poking my chest out a little further, just knowing I had pleased my father.
>
> I don't care how old you are as a father and I don't care how old your children are, whether they're thirty or three, they are not too old or too young for you to sit down in front of them, eye to eye, and say, "I want to tell you something. I'm your father [or mother], and I love you, I am pleased with you, I'm always going to be in your corner, and God has a plan for your life." If you can tell a little boy or girl or an adult man or woman those four things, you will not believe how it will impact them.

When my kids were young, I had a Saturday morning tradition. I would load them all up in the old van and take them to the donut shop and get them all sugared up and ready for the day's activities. Even as a grandfather, I still enjoy that same tradition. Several months ago, I wanted to have some one-on-one time with my four-year old granddaughter, so I picked her up and we headed to the Happy Donut Shop. (Don't you love that name?) Sawyer has beautiful long, blonde hair and piercing blue eyes, and everything in her life is pink—everything! So, she ordered pink donuts and pink milk!

As Sawyer chomped down on one of her donuts, I snapped this picture.

Now, to me, that looks like a little girl on a serious hunger mission. And when she finished that bite, she looked up at me, all serious, and here's what she said:

"I like to fart!"

She really said that! And the reason she said it is because she has two older brothers and a father who are terrible influences in her life when it comes to things like that!

So how in the world does that story relate to the power of the spoken blessing, and in particular to the letter we'll be writing in this chapter? Well, it has everything to do with it. Sawyer is a blessing to me. She's a treasure in my life; and as long as I have these funny stories locked in my memory bank here in my brain, I have the kind of ammo to write this kind of letter.

So, what exactly is a blessing? First, let me share with you what is not. I got into a crowded elevator the other day; and as the door closed, someone let out a big sneeze. What followed sounded like a machine gun burst of "God bless you, God bless you, God bless you!" It's amazing that we've reduced this powerful word, "blessing," to the word we say after someone sneezes.

So, what is the real meaning of that word? Again, as a follower of Christ, my inclination is to turn to God's Word; so that's where I went for the definition. For those of you who are of a different faith or no faith, just know we will be using that definition for this chapter; however, if you will stick with us, I know there are rich nuggets you will be able to glean from it—especially as I describe the four parts of "the blessing" and how you can impart them to your family.

Psalm 1 talks about a man who is blessed (has the favor of God over his life) as he delights in, meditates on, and follows the law of the Lord. We all want the favor of our parents; after all, they're the ones who will buy us a car and send us to college. We want the favor of our boss because he's the one who will hopefully give us a raise. Yet none of that compares with the favor of God, who wants to bless us and shower us with good things.

One day as I was reading in Psalm 1, I looked down in the footnotes and saw what I consider a practical, biblical definition of the word "blessed": "The happy condition of those who love God, serve God, and obey God, and who put their trust fully in Him." To "bless" someone, then, means to give or pronounce the favor of God over their life.

Note that it's not just about being happy, because happiness is an emotion; and just like any emotion, it can change. Rather, the happiness we're speaking of here is an inner peace and security of knowing that no matter what happens in your life, God is in control.

Back when I was putting the final touches on this message for my original *Tackle Box* series for *Letters from Dad*, I took a little break one afternoon and went to my favorite grocery store, which happens to have a wonderful deli. The last thing I had written on my computer before I took a break was this: "Share with the men Proverbs 10:22: *It is the blessings of the Lord that make you rich, and He adds no sorrow to it.*" I also wrote, "Men, when you wake up each morning and you take the first breath into your lungs, remember that it's a gift from God." After writing those words, I headed to the grocery store.

As I entered the store, I grabbed a cart and started pushing it quickly down the aisle. I buzzed past the fish market in the deli, and I heard a guy yell out, "Sir, I love your hat!" I stopped my cart, took off my hat, and read the words, "I Love My Kids." I looked up at him and said, "I really do love my kids, and I love my family." He smiled and said, "I have some shrimp on sale. Would you like to have some?" What a great gimmick that was—he was a fantastic salesman! As he was wrapping my shrimp, he said, "Sir, every day when I get up and I take that first breath of air in my lungs, I thank God that he blessed me with a family." Oh, my goodness! I realized he had stolen the words from my computer screen! Looking at his name tag, I said, "Doug, did you know that it is the blessings of God that make you rich?" I thought he was going to jump over the meat market counter. He said, "Could you repeat that for me? Wait just a moment; I'm going to write it down." I smiled and repeated it as he wrote it down. Then I thanked him for his service, took my shrimp, and went out of the store—and I laughed. I could not believe that God had given me such a tangible affirmation of the teaching on the blessing.

Before we get into writing the letter, let's look at a concept in the Old Testament called "the blessing." I'm forever indebted to John Trent and Gary Smalley, who wrote the book, *The Blessing*, and for their excellent insight into this Old Testament concept. If you go back to the book of Genesis and look at the examples of Abraham,

Isaac, and Jacob, you'll see them bestowing a special blessing over their children. There are four basic components of the blessing, and all four were demonstrated over and over in the life of Christ.

The first part of the blessing is physical touch. Let's look at the power of the physical touch through the eyes of a leper in Matthew 8:1-3: "When Jesus came down from the mountainside, large crowds followed him. A man with leprosy came and knelt before Him and said, 'Lord, if you're willing, you can make me clean.' Jesus reached out and touched the man. 'I am willing,' he said. 'Be clean!'" I'm speaking specifically to men here when I say that your wife, your children, and your grandchildren need the warmth of your loving touch. Of course, it also applies to women, but they are already more inclined to give that much-needed touch!

The second part of the blessing is speaking words of high praise and value. As I was growing up, I never felt the pain of insecurity or bad self-image because my mom was always telling me how much she loved me and how handsome I was. Oh, there were warnings with those blessings. For example, when I was in high school and I had an occasional hot date, my mom would look me in the eyes and she would say, "Son, I see mischief in your eyes. Gregory Lee, I know you're up to something and it's not good. I can see it! Now tonight, I want you to act as nice as you can!" And I can still remember her saying these next words, which would always get to me: "God is watching you!" Oh man! That's not what I wanted to hear before I went on a date! Men and women, speak those words of high praise and value to those you love.

Item number three in the blessing is picturing a special future. Listen to the words that God spoke to us in Jeremiah 29:11: "'*I know the plans I have for you,' declares the Lord. 'Plans to prosper you and not to harm you. Plans to give you a hope and a future.'"* Wow! That's the kind of promises God makes to us!

The last part of the blessing is active commitment. God says to you, "I love you. I died for you. I'll never leave you. I will never, ever forsake you." I'd like to share with you a little saying that has served me well with my kids and my grandkids, and it gives you an example of how you can speak words of both high value and active commitment to your children and grandchildren. It goes like this: "I am yours; you are mine, and I will love you forever."

I had taught my little granddaughter that; and when we got home from the donut shop one day, she went up to her mom and said, "Mom, I am yours, you are mine, and I'll love you forever." I was so excited to hear her say that! Her papa had taught her how to bless someone!

Now let's put all four components together and look at an example of how you might bestow a blessing on your child or your grandchild. You would start with physical touch, perhaps by putting your hand on their shoulder and looking them in the eye. Then you might say:

> Son, you're a very bright young man and you have many wonderful qualities. I love the way you watch over your sister and make your bed in the morning without even being told. I love to watch you play sports and am proud to see your determination to do your best. You are a huge blessing to your mother and me. I know you will grow up to be a wonderful husband, a great father, and a man of impeccable character. I want you to know that I will always be yours, you will always be mine, and I will love you forever.

Question: How different would our world be if every child had someone speaking these kinds of words into their life? I believe it would **change the world**!

I had been searching for a way to help people determine whether they had received the blessings from their parents, and I came up with this little checklist called "The Blessing Quiz."

The Four-Part Blessing	The Ten Most Powerful Words In the English Language
• It begins with a 1. Meaningful Touch • It continues with 2. Spoken Words of High Value • It paints a 3. Picture of a Special Future • It's based on an 4. A/C Active Commitment	(Use them with your spouse, children, business associates and friends!) 1. You 6. New 2. Easy 7. Discovery 3. Save 8. Results 4. Money 9. Proven 5. Love 10. Guarantee *Research by Henry J. Taylor

The Blessing Quotient Quiz

Blessings	Mom	Dad
1. Meaningful Touch		
2. Spoken words of high value		
3. Picture of a Special Future		
4. A/C Active Commitment		
Total		

Grand Total:

The four parts of the blessing are listed at the top, and down below you see the quiz. Just put a check in the boxes if you received that particular component of the blessing from either your mom or dad, or both. When you're finished, add up the number of checks and place it in the box to mark your score.

For most people, taking this quiz serves as a moment of great reflection. For some, there are tears of excitement and joy as they thank God for the high marks they've given their parents. For others (like me), there is a sense of real sadness, or even tears.

Here's how I scored my quiz: Mom, 4; Dad, 0. However, as I worked through the issues dealing with my dad, I realized that my father actually did need to have one check—because he had been actively committed to me. He came to my football games and the important events of my life; and for that, I'm thankful.

I will never forget talking to a group of about thirty business leaders. After I gave the quiz, I asked them to raise their hand if they were able to put checkmarks in all eight boxes, and I worked down from there. Finally, I asked, "How many of you got zero?" Sadly, two hands went up.

For many of us, giving the blessing to our wives and our children and grandchildren is hard because we didn't get it from one or both of our parents. But just because we didn't get it, that doesn't mean we can't give it; and that's what we're learning to do in this journey together. No matter how your parents scored, I highly encourage you to be intentional about ensuring that your kids would be able to check all four boxes under your column (Mom or Dad) if they were to take this quiz in the future.

I had to learn that God, my heavenly Father, has given me every spiritual blessing. I found that in Ephesians 1:3 (NIV), where it says, "Praise be to the God and Father of our Lord Jesus Christ, who has blessed us in the heavenly realms..." with a few spiritual blessings? No, "...with every spiritual blessing in Christ." God wants you to ask Him for His blessing. He's a loving father who has the unlimited capacity to bless.

Now it's time to have some fun together as we move into our writing assignment. We'll be writing the "I Remember When..." letter. If you have children, I strongly suggest you start with your oldest child; if you don't have children, you might want to write this letter to your parents. Or you may remember what Peyton Manning, the two-time Super Bowl quarterback, did—he wrote to his coaches and fellow players. You might want to do something like that.

To help you get started, I put together a list of memories you may have had that will be simple for you to recall. This letter is perfect for any occasion. These memories stored in written form will be a treasured gift remembered—forever!

- I remember when I was told "You are going to be a father."
- I remember the reason why we named you ____
- I remember these special things about the day you were born
- I remember special moments of you like:

  1. a special birthday
  2. your first day of school
  3. learning to swim
  4. the first time you rode a bicycle
  5. losing a tooth
  6. the day your dog died
  7. when you were sick, had a broken arm, etc..
  8. when you learned to ski
  9. the day you trusted Christ as Savior
  10. the day you were Baptized
  11. leaving for camp
  12. starting Junior High
  13. starting High School

14. made the drill team
15. getting your first job
16. went on your first date
17. your graduation
18. playing a sport
19. our favorite vacation/trip
20. learning to drive
21. going off to college
22. the time I was MOST proud of you was
23. you told us you were engaged
24. the day you walked down the aisle
25. you told me "you are going to be a grandparent"
26. a special Christmas or Thanksgiving

This list is endless—keep going!

You won't be writing long remembrances; in fact, you'll be moving through this letter like a freight train. For example, you might say, "I remember the day you came home from the hospital." "I remember that beautiful ballerina dress you wore. You were always my ballerina." "I remember your little brother driving you absolutely mad." "I remember the wreck you had when God saved your life." "I remember the camping trips we had." "I remember the costume parties we had." I think you get the picture. When I wrote this letter to my children, they made comments like, "Dad, I didn't think you remembered those things. I had no idea they were so special to you."

As an example, I've included the letter I wrote to my son David. I think it will help you understand my intention. You will also see the simple template that I used to put my thoughts on paper. You can rough out your letter on a yellow pad using that template and then transfer to stationary when you have completed your thoughts.

Sample "I Remember When..." Letter

Dear David,

It's your birthday—your 29th birthday, and that is cause to celebrate and remember the joy and happiness you have brought me.

I remember the moment Mom said, "I have a little surprise. I don't know how to say this, but you are going to be a dad—again." What joy filled my soul as I dreamed of maybe having the son I had always wanted.

I remember the first time I held you and looked into your eyes. I always love saying your name—David Gregory Vaughn. The word "David" means "**Beloved of God,**" and you certainly are that.

I remember your first day of school when a little girl named Anna Mary Marsh Pickens came running up to you and gave you a big kiss. You were mortified.

I remember happy weekends when we would pack our old van and head off camping with our neighbors and friends.

I remember, when you were just four, leading you in a prayer of salvation and getting to baptize you.

I remember how terrible you were at soccer—you had no interest in anything but picking the wild flowers on the field.

I remember your first football game and how amazed we were. You were ***the leader*** on the field. Your strong character began to emerge and the coaches loved you. They saw what I always saw—your potential for greatness. I have ***never*** doubted your ability to accomplish great things.

I remember the thrill of seeing you pole vault at the state championship in Austin. Every time you cleared the bar I would scream, "That's my son!" I was then, and am now, shameless in my pride for you.

I remember, with sadness but pride, when you graduated from Tech. I knew things were about to change between you and me—you were on your own.

I guess I could go on forever remembering the joys you have brought me. I look with daily excitement to the future memories we will have together.

Always remember my deep love for you. Always remember that my life is so much richer because of you.

Love forever,

DAD

Gregory Lee Vaughn

6/23/08

The "I Remember When..." Template

Dear ____________________

This day, ____________________, I have cause to celebrate and remember the joy and happiness you have brought me.

I remember ____

I remember ____

I remember ______________________________________

I remember ______________________________________

I remember ______________________________________

I remember ______________________________________

I remember ______________________________________

I remember ______________________________________

I remember ______________________________________

I guess I could go on forever remembering the joys you have brought me. I look with daily excitement to the future memories we will have together.

Always remember my deep love for you. Always remember that my life is so much richer because of you.

Love forever,

(Your Name Here)

(Date)

Now it's time to determine how and when you'll be delivering your letter. I love the idea of reading it out loud to your family member or whomever you've written to.

In the next chapter, we'll look at "The Power of Leaving a Visual Legacy."

CHAPTER SIX READER RESPONSE

- Choose the person you want to receive the "I Remember When…" letter.
- Review the template and ideas you see in this chapter. Copy it onto your own practice paper, or you can write directly in the book if you wish.
- Fill in the blanks with your thoughts and memories of that person.
- Once you have completed the list, you can transfer all you have written to some nice stationery. Again, please use your own handwriting, even if it's just a couple of sentences as a P.S. at the bottom of the page.
- Pick the date, time, and place for delivery. I suggest reading it aloud. Verbal praise reinforces your intent and will bless that person greatly.

CHAPTER SIX VIPS

1. For the purposes of this book, we have used the biblical definition of the word "blessed" as: "The happy condition of those who love God, serve God, and obey God, and who put their trust fully in Him." To "bless" someone, then, means to give or pronounce the favor of God over their life.
2. The concept of "the blessing" in the Old Testament is made up of four basic components:
   - physical touch;
   - speaking words of high praise and value;
   - picturing a special future, like God did for us in Jeremiah 29:11: "'*I know the plans I have for you,' declares the Lord. 'Plans to prosper you and not to harm you. Plans to give you a hope and a future.'*"
   - active commitment (e.g., "I am yours; you are mine, and I will love you forever").
3. The "I Remember When…" letter, to be written to your children, your parents, or anyone else you want to bless, is simply a list of memories you have about that person, which lets them know how special they are to you.

CHAPTER SEVEN

The Power of a Visual Legacy

A *Story to Inspire*:

[Note: Our subject for this chapter—"The Power of a Visual Legacy"—is heavily played out in the Bible, so I lean a little more heavily into the Christian viewpoint here. If that's not your worldview, please bear with me, as you will be able to glean powerful distinctions about leaving a visual legacy from the illustrations I use.]

No one has to remind you that we live in a visual world. Experts tell us that, on average, we're bombarded with around 5,000 ads and brand exposures a day. When you then consider all the exposures we get from our smartphones, computers, tablets, and TVs, you can see that we are simply overwhelmed with visual images.

Not long ago, I was reading from a devotional book called *Jesus Is Calling* by Sarah Young. As a Christian, I love this quote Sarah gave: "The curse of this age is the overstimulation of our senses, which locks out our awareness of God." It's true. Our minds are so full of "stuff" and the busyness of life that we fail to see or hear

God's voice. That's why I feel it's important that we be reminded of what I believe—that God is the creator of our visual world. He spoke, "*Let there be light*," and the darkness was dispelled.

I'm convinced that God still speaks to us through His creation every day. When it rains, all we have to do is look up into the sky and see His beautiful rainbow—our reminder of His promise to never again destroy the earth with a flood. Or we can go to the beach with our kids and see God's revelation of Himself through the power of the waves. The psalmist says it this way: "*The heavens declare the glory of God. The skies proclaim the work of His hands*" (Psalm19:1, NIV). Psalm 147:4 (NIV) tells us, "*He determines the number of the stars and calls them each by name.*"

The Bible says in Matthew 10:30 that God even knows the number of hairs on our head [or lack thereof], and in Isaiah 43:1 it says He knows each of us by name. Aren't those amazing facts? According to the Bible, we are His creation, and He loves us!

Let's look at a passage from my favorite book of the Old Testament, the book of Joshua. I just love the motivational and inspirational way the book opens. God says, "*Moses, my servant is dead.*" I suspect God's people were all thinking the same thing: ***What in the world is going to happen to us now?*** Here's the big picture: For forty years, the Jews had wandered in the wilderness after leaving Egypt, and they were all gathered at the Jordan River ready to go into the Promised Land. It was the Super Bowl moment; and their starting quarterback had been knocked out and the B-teamer, a guy named Joshua, had been called up for duty. I'm sure there were questions: ***Can Joshua really do this? Does he have the power and the wisdom to help us conquer our enemies in the land that God had promised us?*** I suspect even Joshua may have had doubts.

Let me ask you a question: Are there times when you fall into discouragement or depression? I do. Sometimes the pressures of this life overwhelm me, and I need a big dose of encouragement to get me through those times. We're about to see some encouraging words from God that I believe we can take to the bank. I call it God's Pregame 101.

Let's look at Joshua 1:5. You can almost envision God, the head coach, putting his arm around Joshua and saying these words to him (paraphrased): "Look, Joshua, no one will be able to stand against you all the days of your life. As I was with Moses, so I'll be with you. I will never, ever leave you or forsake you." And now we're about to read something very rare in the Bible. Obviously, when God gives us a command, I believe we're to listen to and act on that command; and when He repeats it twice in two verses, it's like He's putting a double exclamation mark at the end. However, we're about to see where He repeats the same thing *three times in four verses*!

> Joshua 1:6: *Be strong and courageous, because you will lead these people to inherit the land I swore to their ancestors to give them.*
>
> Joshua 1:7: *Be strong and very courageous.*
>
> Joshua 1:9: *Have I not commanded you? Be strong and courageous. Do not be afraid; do not be discouraged, for the Lord your God will be with you wherever you go.*

It is my strong belief that the same God who gave Joshua that promise has given it to you. He has promised to walk with you on every lonely, painful journey of your life, every moment of disappointment; and He says to you, "Don't worry; don't be afraid, for I'm with you."

Now the tension in the story begins to build. Joshua 3:7 says, "*And the Lord said to Joshua, 'Today, I will begin to exalt you in the eyes of all Israel, so they may know that I am with you as I was with Moses.'*"

Allow me to turn the camera on in your mind's eye for just a moment. Let's visualize the scene together. It was springtime in Israel. The Jordan River was at flood levels. It was like a mighty sea before them and there was no way in the world they could cross it. Then God gave Joshua the game plan. He told Joshua to have the priests take the Ark of the Covenant and walk into the water; and when their feet touched the water, it would immediately pull back and the riverbed would be dry. And it happened just as the Lord said it would; all two million people were able to go safely to the other side! Then God told Joshua (in Joshua 4:2) to choose twelve men from among the people, one for each tribe, and tell them to take up twelve stones from the middle of the Jordan and take them to the other side, to where they would be spending the night.

Now, who do you think Joshua would have chosen for that task? Remember, they were not to pick up just any little stone. Each man was to "take up a stone on his shoulder" (vs. 5), as they were to make a memorial with them that would last even to this day. So, Joshua would have chosen the biggest, strongest dude in each tribe and told them, "Go get the biggest stones in the riverbed." Let's look at verses 5-7:

> *...and [Joshua] said to them, "Go over before the ark of the Lord your God into the middle of the Jordan. Each of you is to take up a stone on his shoulder, according to the number of the tribes of the Israelites, to serve as a sign among you. In the future, when your children ask you, 'What do these stones mean?' tell them that the flow of the Jordan was cut off before*

the ark of the covenant of the Lord. When it crossed the Jordan, the waters of the Jordan were cut off. These stones are to be a memorial to the people of Israel forever.

So, what is the application for us today? No matter what your view of the Bible is, I hope you can recognize that the letters we are writing will be like stones of remembrance to our families. They will remind them: (1) of our love for them, and (2) of our commitment to them. Your letters will be like those stones left on the banks of the Jordan River.

My wife Carolyn has a wonderful gift for creating visual legacies in our home. She keeps us focused on the things that matter. As I was preparing this chapter on the power of visual legacy, I took a little walk through our home to see what I could discover. The first thing I noticed was the number of roosters we had our home. I counted twenty-eight roosters, but what I saw more of were crosses and plaques and photos—lots and lots of photos.

I walked down our hallway, and there was a beautiful display of photos and a plaque that read, "As for me and my house, we will serve the Lord." I walked further down the hallway to our bedroom, where the walls are filled with family photographs. When I sit at our dining room table, I see a large frame that lists the fruits of the Spirit. I think Carolyn is trying really hard to remind me of the fruits of the Spirit because right in front of my throne (my bathroom), I can look up and see another fruit-of-the-Spirit display. Carolyn has placed all these items in our home to remind us of what we stand for and how we are meant to live our lives.

We humans are strongly visual in nature. That's how God has wired us; and I want to encourage you today not to let the god of this world, the devil, steal your mind and pollute it with filthy images that can destroy you. Rather, fill it with the things that remind you of God's goodness and His grace.

When I started *Letters from Dad*, I had just upgraded from my first "mobile" phone. My grandson looked at that phone not long after and said, "Grandpa, that's the coolest phone I've ever seen. When did you get a satellite phone?" I had moved from my "satellite phone" to a fancy new flip phone, but that thing wouldn't even take a picture. Today, we hold in our hands amazing tools for leaving a visual legacy. They're called smartphones, but actually they're super computers.

I spoke to my daughter Brooke the other day, and she had two screaming children in the background around her. She was trying and failing to continue a calm conversation with me as she wrangled her two little girls at the same time. When we finished, I texted a photo of her and those beautiful children with these words: "I know you have the hardest job in the world. You're doing a great job. You're the best! Love, Dad." Now, how do you think that might've encouraged her? These are the types of things we need to learn to communicate with our family using the power of the visual medium.

A few years ago I had the opportunity to be on Dave Ramsey's television program. Dave has been a great supporter of *Letters from Dad*; and when I was on his program, he asked me a question that really made me think. He asked, "What experience in your background helped birth the concepts of *Letters from Dad*?" No one had ever asked me that question, so I had to think about it. After reflection, I was confident that these concepts came from decades of producing family video biographies. You see, God has given me a wonderful company called Grace Ministries; but what I really do for a living is produce family video biographies. Over the years, I've produced more than a hundred of these kinds of movies; and it was there in the trenches that I learned what a godly legacy looked like and what it didn't look like.

I have a question for you today; it's one of those "wow" kind of questions: What if you could push a button and on the screen in front of you would appear your great, great, great grandfather? I mean, could you even imagine what that would be like—to meet him and for him to share his history and the events that shaped his life? Let me stretch you even further. What if you were to hear words like, "Though I've never met you, please know that I prayed for you. I prayed that you would come to know the great God I have served all the days of my life." Well, of course we have all the tools we need today to make that happen for our great, great, great grandchildren—the digital camera and the smartphone.

Let me encourage you to take these tools and preserve your heritage for future generations. Video your mom, your dad, and your grandparents. Record your family's history and especially ask them questions about matters of faith, hope, and love because future generations desire greatly to know your roots and the faith journey of your family.

The first video biography I ever produced was about the hero of my life—a little lady named Wanda Fay Vaughn, my godly mom. She was very ill at the time. I knew I didn't have much longer with her, and that weighed heavily on my mind. I was in the hospital one night, just hanging out with her; and we were watching one of those great biographies on the history channel.

I turned to my mom and said, "Someone needs to do one of those movies on your life." She laughed and said, "Why in the world would you say that, Son?" "Because I need to be able to introduce you, Mom, to the future generations of my family." Driving back to Dallas, I felt God say, "Greg, I've equipped you make that movie. You do it." So, I did. I produced one of those A&E quality movies about my mom's life; and I kept it a secret, not telling anyone in our family. But when Mom died, I felt it was time to show the movie. I had the honor of speaking at her memorial service last. Allow me to paint the picture of the moment. My mom was lying peacefully in the casket when I said, "It just doesn't seem quite right that Mom shouldn't say a few words to us today." Then I said to the sound man, "Push the button," and Mom roared up onto the big screen.

You could see the shock and surprise on the faces of the people in the audience, and many told me later that the hair was standing up on the back of their neck. Then it happened—like a great preacher, my mom delivered a three-point sermon on the importance of faith, hope, and love. As she was closing that pep talk to us, she said, "God has already given me my address in heaven, so grab a pen and some paper. I'll be living at the corner of Hallelujah and Praise Streets. Don't forget to come and see me." I saw the power of the visual legacy, and I knew then that I would spend the rest of my life creating ministry tools like that for families.

Now I'd like for you to meet a friend of mine. (He was also a friend of Tony's and was even his business partner as well.) He is no longer with us; he's with Jesus. His name is Zig Ziglar, and I had the great honor of producing his video biography. Zig was an amazing man, a wonderful father and grandfather. I think he was perhaps the greatest motivational speaker and author of all time. While I was filming him, he told me he wanted to share his testimony of Christ to his family and future generations. This is what he said:

> I met my Savior on July the Fourth, 1972, when we invited Sister Jessie, an elderly Black lady, to spend the weekend in our home. She walked in talking about Christ and she walked out talking about Christ, and for the entire time that's all she talked about. And if she said it one time, she said it a hundred times: "God's been waiting on you a long time." That's when I committed my life to Christ. That's when my career exploded. That's when my love for my wife grew even more; and I've

> always loved her from the time I first saw her. When Sister Jesse got through with me that evening, I have to tell you, I was so excited about knowing Christ as my Lord and Savior.
>
> I want to leave you with one thought that I believe will make you a better person: I believe with all my heart that you can have everything in life you want if you just help enough other people get what they want. And I'm going to conclude by saying, "When you get to heaven, I'm going to be welcoming you at the door."

Isn't that just amazing? I call this "Your Story for God's Glory," and we'll be talking more about how to do that in the final chapter.

Now, let's talk about your writing assignment for this chapter. You're going to be writing a thank-you letter to your parents. If they are no longer with you, I'll show you how you can do that. First, though, I encourage you to look at photos of your parents. When I do that, I'm flooded with memories of the sacrifices they made for our family. These photos will serve as springboards to help you write a letter of honor and blessing to your parents. You're going to say, "Thank you, Mom, and thank you, Dad, for all you did."

One of the founding members of *Letters from Dad* was a man named Clint Regehr. Clint wrote his letter to his father for his eightieth birthday. I think it serves as a beautiful example of the kind of letter you might want to write.

> Wow! Eighty years of celebrating life! I wanted to let you know some important things that I have appreciated about you over the years. First of all, thank you for loving me the way you do. I know that you have always honored God and have brought me up to know the truth. Second, thank you for loving Mom the way you did. It gave me an example of faithfulness and devotion in my own marriage. It made me

feel secure as a child growing up in a home where I didn't have to worry about my parents' stability. When I look at our three-generation picture, it always makes me feel emotional because of what we all stand for. Dad, I love you and honor you and your life on this special eightieth birthday. May God continue to bless your life richly as you've blessed mine.

Much love, from Clint, Carol, Jenny, Jordy, and Brittany.

I hope you noticed how he integrated photos in his letter to enhance the power of his words. Frankly, I would need some help doing that; but hopefully we can all write letters and maybe even enclose copies of a few of our favorite photos.

You may be thinking, *What if my parents are deceased?* Write to them anyway, as if they were alive. Write them a tribute letter and send a copy to your kids because it will be a treasure for them to read your words of remembrance, and it will give your kids insight into your relationship with your parents.

I've had men say, "Greg, it's just too painful for me to write that kind of letter. I can't do it." Your relationship may have been very difficult, even non-existent. If you can't write that kind of letter, I understand. But perhaps it could be a letter of forgiveness or reconciliation, a steppingstone to restore that relationship. Move as God moves you.

Regardless, there is someone in your life to whom you need to say thank you. Perhaps it's a mentor, an aunt, an uncle, a grandparent, or a sibling. As you move into your writing assignment, please feel free to write any style of letter you want. If you get stuck on the letter, just remember—you had the skill to write both the "I Am Blessed" letter and the "I Remember When…" letters. You can write this one, too.

In the next chapter, we'll be looking at how to leave a legacy of prayer.

CHAPTER SEVEN READER RESPONSE

- First, take a few moments to reflect on the subjects of your thank-you letter. If it's your parents, as suggested, or someone else, quickly jot down all the things that are brought to mind.
- Now, expand on those thoughts. Give examples of what they did and what you learned. How did it impact your life? This exercise may be a little challenging at first, but you will be shocked at how your ideas flow once you begin to write. Don't worry about grammar, punctuation, or spelling; just get it down on paper.
- Once you have completed the rough draft, transfer all you have written to some nice stationery. As before, use your own handwriting, even if it's not that good.
- Here's the fun part: This is setting you up for the "visual" part of a legacy. Take a few moments with your phone and record yourself reading that letter to the subject. Don't just use audio; flip that camera around and speak directly, just as if that person were right in front of you. If that seems too intimidating, then be sure to include photos of you and the subject over the years. You could do both! This will help trigger those memories and foster the closeness that can be lost in the busyness of life.
- Pick the date, time, and mode of delivery. Since this is a little different than the previous presentations, you can be creative. Depending on the circumstances, this may be a presentation that would be read and then shown directly to the subject or family group. If the situation is delicate, this could be sent by mail.

CHAPTER SEVEN VIPS

1. God is the creator of our visual world. He spoke, "*Let there be light*," and the darkness was dispelled. God still speaks to us through His creation every day. "*The heavens declare the glory of God. The skies proclaim the work of His hands*" (Psalm19:1, NIV).
2. The same God who gave Joshua the promise in Joshua 1:9 has given it to you. "*Have I not commanded you? Be strong and courageous. Do not be afraid; do not be discouraged, for the Lord your God will be with you wherever you go.*"
3. Use tools like a digital camera and your smartphone to preserve your heritage for future generations. You can video your mom, your dad, and your grandparents. Record your family's history; and especially ask them questions about matters of faith, hope, and love because future generations desire greatly to know your roots and the faith journey of your family. Feel free to contact Greg directly with help in this area.
4. Write a thank-you letter to your parents. Looking at photos first may flood you with memories of the sacrifices they made for your family and serve as springboards to help you write a letter of honor and blessing to your parents.

CHAPTER EIGHT

The Power of Prayer

A Story to Inspire:

I ask your indulgence, once again, as we delve into the tenets of Christianity and the Bible, this time to talk about the power of prayer. Please know that there are powerful truths tucked away for you in this chapter, no matter what you believe, especially as we talk about the indelible impact you can have on your family by writing the final letter of your life.

I was watching one of my favorite television programs recently, *America's Funniest Home Videos*, and there was a great clip that reminded me about the importance of prayer.

Let me paint the scene for you, if I can. It was filmed during a Vacation Bible School at a small church. All the parents and grandparents had turned out in big numbers for the closing event. Everyone had their video cameras in hand, ready for action. One of the moms had been informed that her daughter would be answering a question, so she had dressed her daughter up and pulled her hair back in pigtails in order to feature her little face. The teacher told the crowd that they had been studying the story of Jesus turning water into wine. She turned to the group of small children and said, "Sally, would you like to tell everyone the meaning of that story?" Sally thought for a minute and said, "Well, I think the meaning is that when you are home and you run out of wine" (and she said this next part very fervently), "you need to get on your knees and pray and ask God for some more wine."

I think that little girl won the $10,000 that night! She might not have quite had the right meaning behind that miracle, but I wish we all had the same fervent attitude about prayer that she had.

In my first *Letters from Dad* group, when I suggested to the men that we write the final letter of our lives, those guys really wanted to throw their dinner rolls at me. They did not like that suggestion! They asked, "Why in the world would we do that, Greg?" My response to them was, "Men, on the darkest day of our family's life, I think we should step up to the plate and deliver words of faith, hope, love, comfort, and encouragement to them. Let me be honest with you—it takes a man with great courage to write this kind of letter. But for the men who have written it, their lives were never the same. Why? Because they could rest in the fact that the things they wanted to say at the end of their life had been said in their own words and in their own way." Of course, the same goes for women. How inspiring and comforting would it be for moms and grandmothers to express those same kinds of words of faith, hope, and love to their families at the end of their lives?

My friend Bodie Spangler's family received such a letter from his dad after he passed away, and here's what Bodie had to say about the impact it had on his family:

> We were reading through this letter, and it opened with a portion for my mom, encouraging her. I remember hearing Mom read that aloud, and then she started reading the part for my sister and for me. It said, "Dear Bodie and Claire, I

want to remind you how pleased I am with the adults you've become." He talked about some things that had happened in our lives recently, my graduation from the academy and some things that my sister had done. Then he said, "I want to remind you that no matter what happens, I love you. I'm your father, and I love you." Then he closed the letter by saying, "God has a special plan for each one of you." And he started talking about some of the successes in our lives. For me, he said, "Bo, your Annapolis education will serve you well for the rest of your life." I remember one thing my father had told us throughout our lives was that no matter what happened, he was always going to be in our corner. That letter, for me, was the opportunity I had to hear those words one last time. "I know I'm not here, but I'm still in your corner." The final words from him were, "I'm pleased with you. I love you, I'm for you, and God has a plan for your life."

The last thing in the world the enemy of your soul wants is for you to write the final letter of your life because it's such a powerful letter. I can promise you it will be read over and over again by your spouse, your children, and your grandchildren; and therefore, it deserves your special attention and time. I know the only way most of you will finish this letter is with a great deal of prayer. Therefore, this chapter will focus on two powerful principles of the Bible: the hope of heaven and the power of prayer. We will also look at a number of Scripture verses that will inspire your words as you write to your family.

You may be asking, Greg, why in the world are you so intense about this letter? Why do you have such a sense of urgency? Here's why: A few years ago, just south of Dallas, I was launching a *Letters from Dad* kickoff. The church had been very successful in promoting the event, and there were over eighty men who attended that session. The pastor wanted to personally lead the men. While they were doing their writing assignment for that session, the pastor was taking care of some extra details; so his writing time was cut short, and he wasn't able to finish his letter. The next day, as he was driving home from the church, a truck swerved across the center lane and struck him head on; and my friend, pastor David Edwards was killed. It was a shock to the church. It was a shock to his family! And it crushed the men who were attending the *Letters from Dad* events. The men in his Legacy Group discovered his workbook in his car. They turned to his worksheet, and they found his unfinished letter to his wife. I had the privilege of speaking at the church the following week and had the honor of reading that unfinished letter to his wife and children and the entire church. The words he wrote were simple but powerful, and his wife Lindsey will cherish and treasure them all the days of her life.

That is a very sad story; but it would be even more tragic if not for the eternal hope and confidence his family had in the Scriptures, and especially in one particular passage. Listen to the comforting words that Jesus, the Savior, spoke in John 14:2: "*My Father's house has many rooms; if it were not so, would I have told you that I'm going there to prepare a place for you?*" Where is "there"? The "there" is heaven! Jesus continues in verse 3: "*And if I go and prepare a place for you, I will come back and take you to be with me that you also may be where I am.*" That is the promise Jesus has given us; and He, being God, cannot lie to us. Heaven is a real place where my friend David Edwards is living. Let's add to that the promise of Philippians 3:20: "*But our citizenship is in heaven. And we eagerly await a Savior from there, the Lord Jesus Christ.*"

Before we begin writing, I also want to focus our attention on what it means to leave a legacy of prayer. If there is one thing I want my kids to remember, it's this: "My dad was a praying father. He prayed for me all the days of my life."

Let me encourage you here with a powerful promise from James 5:16: "*The prayer of a righteous person is powerful and effective.*" I love the way the *Living Bible* says this: "*The earnest prayer of a righteous man has great power and wonderful results.*"

As I was working on this chapter, I had just typed out those verses on my computer screen when my cell phone rang. It was a couple I'd known for decades, Mark and Carol Faulkner. They had been in the ministry for years. Mark was on the waiting list for a heart transplant. They were in tears when they called me. Things weren't going well; they had no money, and they were being evicted from their apartment. Measured by earthly standards, their life looked pretty hopeless. But as I listened to them, it was plainly obvious that they were clinging to a firm hope in their Savior. Through their tears, I heard these words: "Greg, God has not abandoned us, and we are confident that He is still in control of our lives." As we were finishing our visit, I asked if I could pray for them. I had never felt so powerless and so inadequate to help someone in all my life. My prayer was very simple because I couldn't find the words to say; but finding the right words for God is of no concern. He simply hears the cries of help from his children's lips. As I came back to my computer after I prayed for them, I saw I Peter 3:12 on my screen. It was a verse that suddenly took on a whole new meaning as I read it: "*For the eyes of the Lord are on the righteous, and his ears are attentive to their prayer.*"

If we ask, He will answer, but not always in the way we want or expect. Sometimes "Yes," sometimes "No," and sometimes He just says "Wait." Mark and Carol's financial needs were miraculously met and their living situation greatly improved. However, Mark's health continued to decline, and a heart transplant soon became impossible. Despite that, Mark's faith never wavered; he was confident that God was in control. As we know, God is not a genie in a lamp that we rub and get three wishes. Sometimes He says, "It's time to come home."

Over the last ten years, I have been mentoring my son, David Vaughn, to take the reins of Grace Ministries. I thought the best way to do that was to put him right next to my office. David can literally hear every conversation I have on the phone; and, conversely, I can hear every conversation he has. That way we're always on the same page with regard to our ministry. Sometimes it gets kind of loud and noisy when we're helping our pastors on the phone throughout the country.

There are times when I hear these words: "Dad, can you help me with something in here?" When I hear those words, no matter what's happening in my world, I hit the pause button on everything. Why? Because my son needs attention. He needs my help. And so it is with God—His eyes and ears are always on us; and when we cry out to Him, He is always there to help us.

What this says is that prayer is important. God uses prayer to heal the hurts in our marriages and in our families. Prayers even have the power to change the hearts and bad attitudes of rebellious teenagers. The older I get, the more I realize I have no power in my life to change people. It only took me fifty years and a lot of pain to learn that lesson. I do have some influence in the lives of my family, and I should use it; but the real power I have is found in the power of God's Holy Spirit as I ask him for good things on behalf of my family.

Psalm 116:1-2 (TLB) gives us the encouragement we need to persist in our prayers to the Lord. "*I love the Lord because He hears my prayers, and He answers them. Because he bends down and listens, I will pray as long as I breathe.*" Colossians 4:2 talks about being devoted in prayer: "*Devote yourself to prayer, being watchful and thankful.*"

One of my daughters has always been a prayer warrior, and she taught me a powerful lesson. When she was about sixteen years old, Brooke came to me and said, "Dad, I've been working all summer as a lifeguard, and I've saved about $1,600. I was wondering if you could help me find a good used car. I added a little money to hers, and we went shopping. She had only three requirements: First, she wanted a white car, which sounded reasonable to me; and she wanted a car that got great gas mileage. You want to know why? Because my kids paid for all their own gas! And finally (and I liked this one), she wanted a CD player in her car so she could play her worship music. We found a good (very used) Nissan that met all her requirements, and I'll never forget seeing the excitement on her face as she ran out the front door and came to grab the keys to ***her*** new car!

Before we drove off, she thanked me. And then she prayed this bold prayer: "Lord, thank you for my new car. Please protect me as I drive it. I pray that it will never, ever fail me mechanically." I started laughing. I thought, *Right! A very used car with 120,000 miles on it, and she's asking God for no mechanical problems?* You know what? We had seven old used cars for all my teenagers in the driveway, and Brooke's was the only car that never broke down! Wow! The power of a praying teenager! It sure did bring conviction to this doubting dad.

We need to realize that we possess the most powerful weapon in the world for our family, and it's called prayer. God tells us this about prayer launched from the heart of a man or woman of God: "*The weapons we fight with are not the weapons of the world. On the contrary, they have divine power to demolish strongholds*" (2 Corinthians 10:4). Our prayers are like a powerful cruise missile blasting out of a submarine beneath the sea. With their guidance system, they arch through the sky; and as I'm sure all of you have seen in the videos, these missiles turn and twist their way down the middle of the street—and with pinpoint accuracy, they annihilate the enemy. Prayer is one of God's greatest gifts to us, and we must become people of prayer!

Before we begin our writing assignment, I would like to share a story that has greatly impacted my life. On January 2, 2006, the small mining town of Sego, West Virginia, was rocked with a mining explosion. Twelve miners died in that tragedy. There was only one survivor; his name was Randall McCloy, Jr. Months later, Randall penned a letter to the families of those who were lost, recounting their last moments together.

> We were worried and afraid, but we began to accept our fate. Junior Toler led us all in the sinner's prayer. We prayed a little longer, then someone suggested that we each write a letter to our loved ones. I wrote a letter to Anna and my children. When I finished writing, I put the letter in Jackie Weaver's lunchbox, where I hoped it would be found. As time went on, I became very dizzy and lightheaded. Some drifted off into what appeared to be a deep sleep, and one person sitting near me collapsed and fell off his bucket. It was clear that there was nothing I could do to help him. The last person I remember speaking to was Jackie Weaver, who reassured me that if it was our time to go, then God's will would be fulfilled. As my trapped coworkers lost consciousness one by one, the room grew still; and I continued to sit and wait, unable to do much else. I have no idea how much time went by before I also passed out from the gas and smoke, awaiting rescue.

Now it's time to write. You're not trapped in a mine, but you do need to write your letter. Let me coach you before you pick up your pen. I don't want you struggling in your mind's eye over some lofty words. Keep it simple, just like the miners did. Just tell your family what's on your heart. Tell them you love them. Remind them of the joy and the happiness they have brought you. Share with them your hope of heaven, encourage them to put their faith in the Savior, and remind them that eternity starts when they join you in heaven.

These are sacred moments. I pray that as you pick up your pen and write from your heart to those you love, God will fill you with His love and mercy; that He will speak through your words of faith, hope, and love; and that it will be an encouragement to your family.

CHAPTER EIGHT READER RESPONSE

Question: If you were to die ***today***, what would your wife, children, and grandchildren hold in their hand ***tomorrow*** that would let them know they were the treasures of your life?
Answer: It will be the final letter of your life!

It doesn't have to be long. Certainly the dying miners in the Sago Mine accident proved that. There is no template, and there is no sample for this letter. This is personal; no one can do it for you. Just open your computer and start writing from your heart to those you love. What are your hopes and dreams for them?

And don't forget to tell them about the things that matter most to ***you***!

There can only be three words to describe such a letter: "a precious heirloom." I have received hundreds of letters from sons, daughters, and spouses thanking me for challenging their lost loved one to write such a letter; it has become priceless to them.

So now, start writing!

CHAPTER EIGHT VIPS

1. Although we don't have the power to change people, we do have some influence in the lives of our family, and we should use it. But the real power we have is found in the power of God's Holy Spirit as we ask Him for good things on behalf of our family. Psalm 116:1-2 (TLB) gives us the encouragement we need to persist in our prayers to the Lord. "*I love the Lord because He hears my prayers, and He answers them. Because he bends down and listens, I will pray as long as I breathe.*"
2. Why would we write a final letter to our family? Because on the darkest day of our family's life, we should step up to the plate and deliver words of faith, hope, love, comfort, and encouragement to them.
3. Keep your final letter to your family simple. Just tell them what's on your heart. Tell them you love them. Remind them of the joy and the happiness they have brought you. Share with them your hope of heaven, encourage them to put their faith in the Savior, and remind them that eternity starts when they join you in heaven.

Conclusion

So, how does your *Legacy Adventure* look so far?

Now that you've read through the book, let's revisit the questions we asked at the beginning:

At the end of your life, what will people say about you?

When that time arrives, what difference will you have made on the lives of others, particularly in the lives of your family and the generations to come?

In other words, what will be your legacy?

Note from Tony: Whether you're still in the Learning or Earning Quadrant or you're in the Reaping or Returning Quadrant, I pray you've been inspired to intentionally and strategically map out your plan for leaving your imprint on the world, and particularly on your family and future generations. Hopefully we've given you some new perspectives and a few aha's and epiphanies along the way about how to accomplish that.

In the Learning Quadrant chapter, for example, you may have been exposed to the concept of *Parental Privilege* for the first time and learned how you can exponentially boost your kids' self-esteem and chances of success by more strategically parenting or grandparenting.

In chapter 2, the Earning Quadrant, you may have been persuaded to think deeper and more strategically about the level of economic stability and direction you're providing for your family and those you lead. Maybe you were prompted to check your money management habits and make sure they are working smartly for you—perhaps even while you sleep.

If you're in the Reaping Quadrant, which we discussed in chapter 3, I'm really hoping you're realizing rewards from the life you've built and that you're impacting the lives of others to another level while you're enjoying that life. I pray we were able to motivate you to live (or continue living) a healthy lifestyle so you can not only enjoy a longer life, but also so you can model healthy living for your family—a very important aspect of leaving a great legacy.

And finally, for those in the Returning Quadrant (chapter four), I hope you came to understand the enormous benefits of decluttering your life and living simply so you can create space for so much more! Can you imagine having the freedom of time and space to enjoy serving others, traveling, investing time with your grandchildren, meditating on God's Word, or so many other worthwhile pursuits that will enhance your legacy? Maybe you've even been inspired to write a book or create a blog to bring about positive change in the lives of others during this quadrant.

It's been a joy to partner with my friend Greg Vaughn on this *Legacy Adventure* as we've presented concepts and ideas—each within our own areas of experience, expertise, and gifting—that will magnify and strengthen the imprint you leave on the world. Now I'll let Greg speak to the thoughts he wants to leave with you concerning the *Letters to Dad* concepts he's presented in his very inspirational part two of the book.

Note from Greg: It has been a pleasure to work with Tony on this project. His insight and energy have been an inspiration to me. Legacy has been a driving force in my life for many years, and I am honored to work with someone who is so like-minded.

I want to encourage all of you to be keenly aware of the power of your words, both spoken and written. They have the power to build up or tear down, to bless and inspire, or to curse and discourage. Your legacy hinges on what you say and do. I strongly encourage you to think carefully before you speak and to not be in haste when you write. A quick tongue and an angry hand leave a legacy of regret.

Remember special occasions; those are excellent opportunities to share words of faith, hope, and love. Just a short note or a simple letter can become a cherished item. We seldom realize the impact simple things can have.

Finally, take time to consider who is the ***hero*** of your life. Have you thought about how you might capture their story and the impact they have had on your life? How can this be shared with future generations? If I can be of any help please let me know.

If you've not done so, please take the time to complete the action steps at the end of each chapter. By completing these activities, you'll come much closer to making a profound impact on the lives of others and creating a lasting legacy of support and inspiration. In the introduction, I (Tony) spoke of my life-changing methodology of *Clarity, Focus*, and *Execution*. In the chapters throughout this book, we've hopefully helped you find clarity about the things you can and should do to take you farther along on your *Legacy Adventure;* and we've given you many ideas to focus on to help you get there. It's now up to you to take the action necessary (execute) to bring substance to your journey.

We hope you will help us spread the word by buying this powerful book as a gift for others so they, too, can embark on the *Legacy Adventure* of their lives and learn how to leave the world a much better place. Imagine, if you will, the immediate impact you could have by sharing this book with the people in your world—your children, friends, neighbors, coworkers, and extended family members. Let's change the world—one person at a time!

And please study the "How We Can Help You" section at the back of the book and reach out to us to explore how we can be of further service to you. You can reach Tony by email at info@tonyjeary.com or by phone at 817-430-9422, and Greg can be reached at greg@grace101.org or 800-527-4014.

We pray you will be blessed beyond measure as you continue on your *Legacy Adventure.*

What We Can Do For You

What Tony Can Do For You

Results Coaching

Advice Matters, if it's the right advice. Having coached the world's top CEOs, published nearly 100 books, and advised over 1,000 clients, Tony has positioned himself with a unique track record to take serious high achievers to a whole new level of results.

Interactive Keynotes

Tony not only energizes, entertains, and educates; he also has his team work strategically and smartly with the event team to make his part, as well as the entire experience, a super win. An hour with Tony often changes people's lives forever and impacts an organization's results immediately. He delivers value, a fun factor, and best practices people can really use.

Strategic Acceleration Facilitation Planning

Tony can do in a single day what takes many others days or even weeks to accomplish. He provides at your fingertips three decades of best practices, processes, and tools for accelerating dramatic, sustained results in any organization.

Collaborative Relationships

We selectively partner with organizations in a *Growth Partnership* arrangement. We supercharge and help winners win more. Most winning leaders know they can always win better and faster by teaming up with the right people, adding the right resources, and becoming clearer on their vision. Our foundational methodology of *Clarity, Focus, and Execution* is deployed in such a way that our partners get the right results faster.

We built a multi-million-dollar think tank seven minutes from DFW Airport called the RESULTS Center (www.resultscenter.co). It is the ultimate destination where teams synergize, powerful

The ultimate think tank: a powerful place for holding strategic clarity and planning meetings

plans are built, and individuals become energized to compress their time to turn visions into reality—often in less time than believed possible.

We have over 30,000 contacts, three decades of proprietary-built tools, multiple investment options, a hand-selected team, and a thirty-year proven track record, all to be leveraged with the right partners. We bring energy (*Vibe*) to the table.

Please visit www.tonyjeary.com as well as www.tonyjearytheresultsguy.com, and then reach out to us at info@tonyjeary.com to discuss what we can do for you.

What Greg Can Do For You

Legacy Coaching

Written and spoken words matter, especially when they are intentional and grounded in purpose, because of the eternal impact they can have. Known across the country as the "Legacy Guy," Greg Vaughn has spent over five decades helping individuals and families capture their stories, values, and purpose for future generations. His legacy work is not just motivational, it's transformational, inspiring thousands to live lives that matter and to pass on what matters most to future generations.

Through Grace Ministries, Greg has produced hundreds of inspirational video resources and has partnered directly with over 80,000 churches. His legacy coaching impact extends far beyond content—it sparks movements that equip people to leave behind more than possessions. It helps them speak to future generations about the things that matter.

Inspirational Presentations

Greg Vaughn doesn't just deliver messages—he delivers movements. As the founder and national leader of Letters from Dad, Greg ignited a men's legacy movement that launched in over 4,000 churches and civic organizations. His best-selling book by the same title continues to equip and challenge fathers to leave written legacies that bless their families for generations.

Greg has been a featured guest on Focus on the Family and The Dave Ramsey Show; and he has appeared in more than **eighty national publications**, including the front page of the *L.A. Times*. Whether he's keynoting a conference or appearing on television, his words resonate because they call people to something deeper—a life worth living and a story worth telling.

Strategic Legacy Tools

Greg Vaughn is a world leader in Family Video Biographies through his company, The Video Biography Company. He pioneered this field with one clear conviction: *"A life worth living is a story worth telling."* His team works with families to preserve their values, stories, and testimonies in a compelling, high-quality video format. These life documentaries are more than interviews; they are legacy experiences.

Greg also produced the award-winning film series *In Search of the Heroes*, bringing to life figures such as Anne Frank, George Washington Carver, Harriet Tubman, and Susan B. Anthony for children around the world. These Emmy Award–winning films have been featured on television and used in over 30,000 schools and libraries, winning every major educational award for historical content.

Collaborative Legacy Relationships

Greg believes that legacy is not a solo journey. He has spent his life collaborating with and coaching individuals in how to record their family history and values for future generations. Through decades of partnerships and visionary storytelling, Greg has helped people across cultures and generations discover what matters most—and how to pass it on.

His heartbeat is not only found in his public work, but also in his personal legacy. Greg is a **father of seven** and a grandfather of nine, living in McKinney, Texas, with his beloved wife Carolyn. He often says that no amount of public success compares to the joy of being a faithful father and grandfather.

Legacy Studio Experience

The ultimate legacy lab: A sacred space for filming life stories, capturing family values, and crafting multigenerational impact. It could be your living room or our private studio, wherever you feel most comfortable.

Greg continues to lead and innovate in legacy communication, leveraging over fifty years of ministry and media production, helping individuals and families craft and deliver legacies that live long after they are gone.

Please visit www.videobiography.com to learn more or reach out to connect with Greg and his team.

Email: greg@grace101.org Phone: 800-527-4014 x0

About the Authors

Tony Jeary has impacted people's success now for over thirty years. Tony likes to win, and he wins by helping others win. He chooses carefully the people and organizations he works with and then goes all in, focusing on what will provide the highest/next-level return on effort. Tony is a prolific author, with most of his 100 titles focused on helping others get *RESULTS Faster!* He and his team work mainly in his unique, private RESULTS Center, located just a few minutes north of DFW Airport, which houses his thirty-plus years of *Best Practices*, courses, and tools.

Greg Vaughn is often referred to as the "Legacy Guy."

Greg is an Emmy-Award-winning film producer who has created inspirational family content through his company, Grace Ministries, for over fifty years.

He founded The Video Biography Company, which has become the world leader in the production of family video biographies.

As the author of the book *Letters from Dad*, he launched a national men's legacy movement that encompassed over 4,000 churches and civic organizations.

Finally, and most proudly, he is the father to seven children and grandfather to nine. He lives in McKinney, Texas, with his wonderful wife Carolyn.